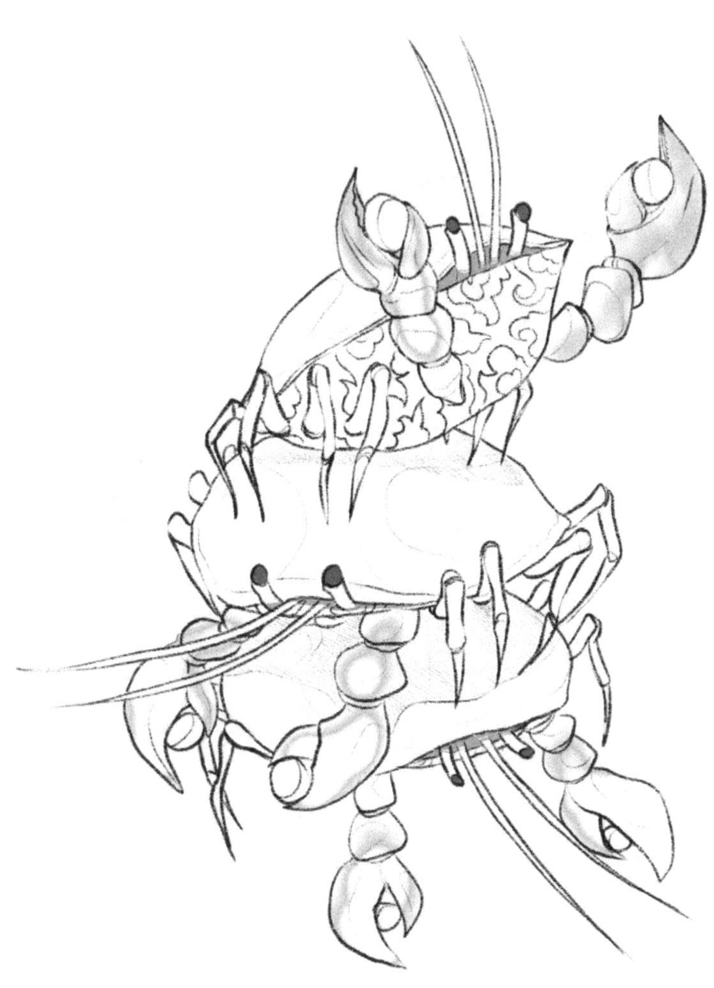

Published by Crane & Wolf Publishing
ISBN-13: 978-1987651119
ISBN-10: 1987651111

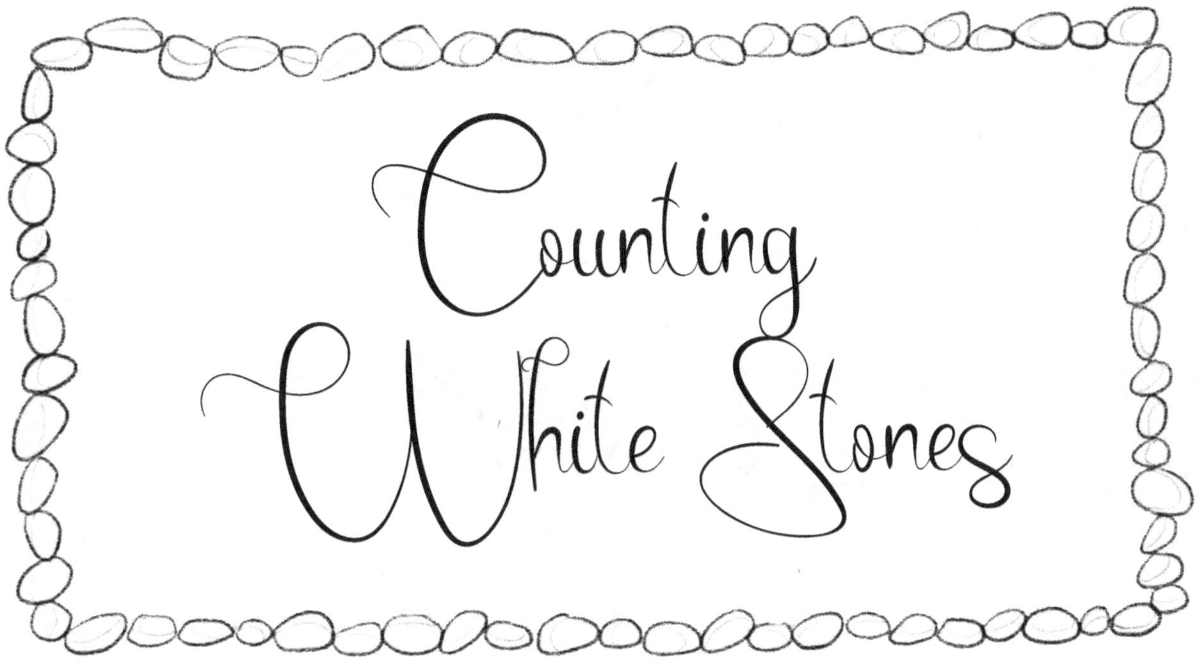

Counting White Stones

The Coloring Book

Illustrated by Saturne Mezzasalma

Based on the story by Chani Petro

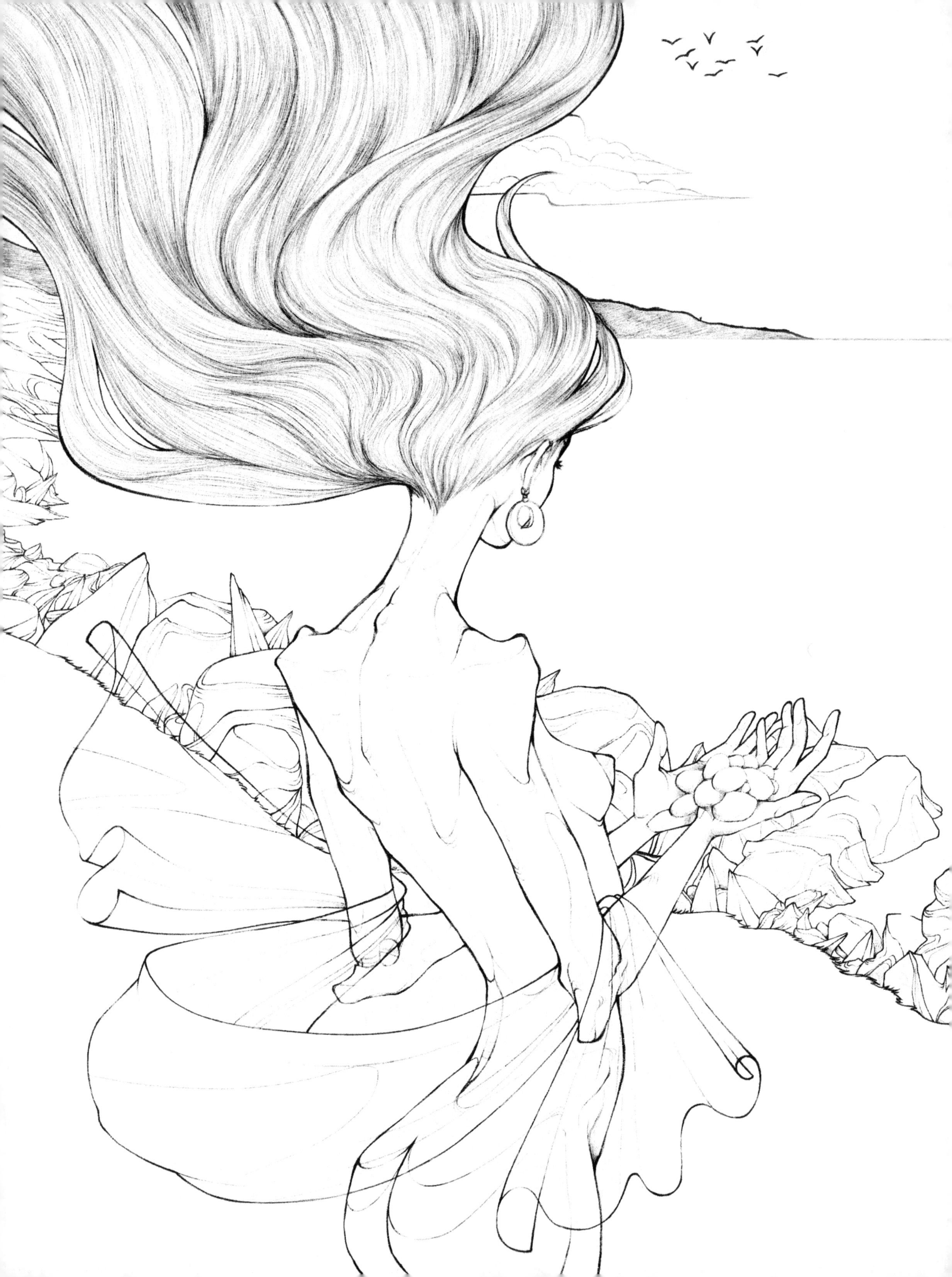

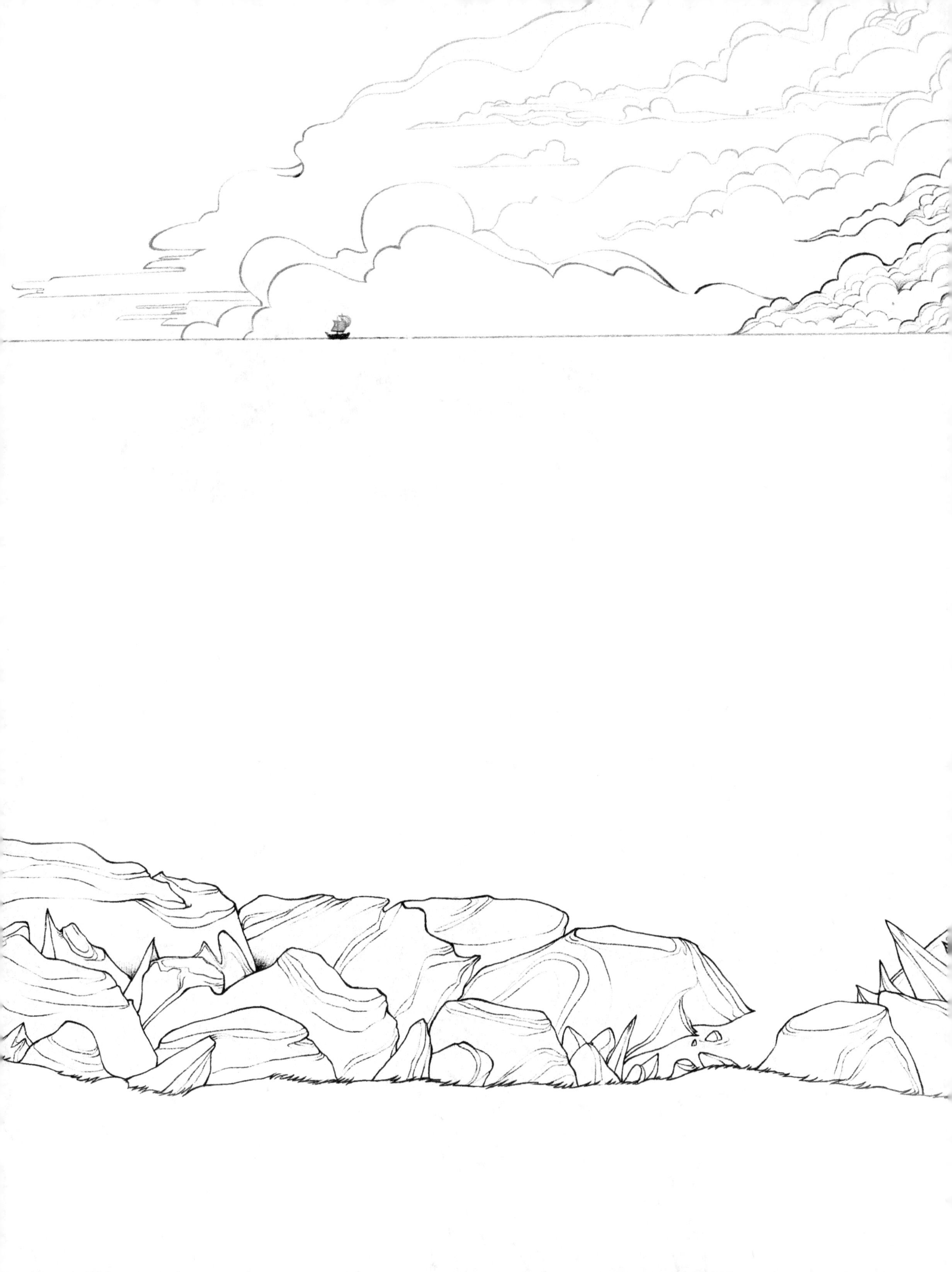

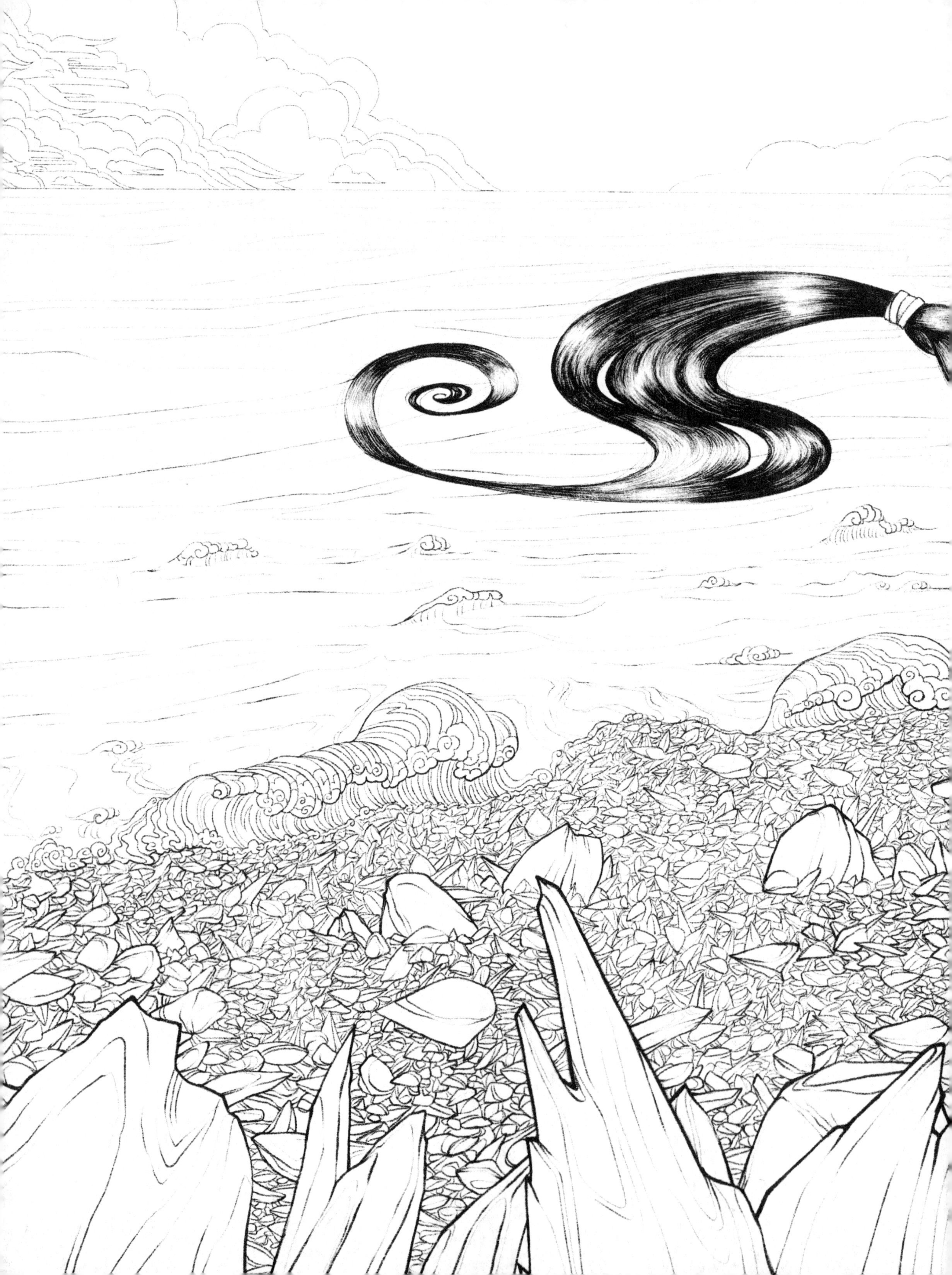

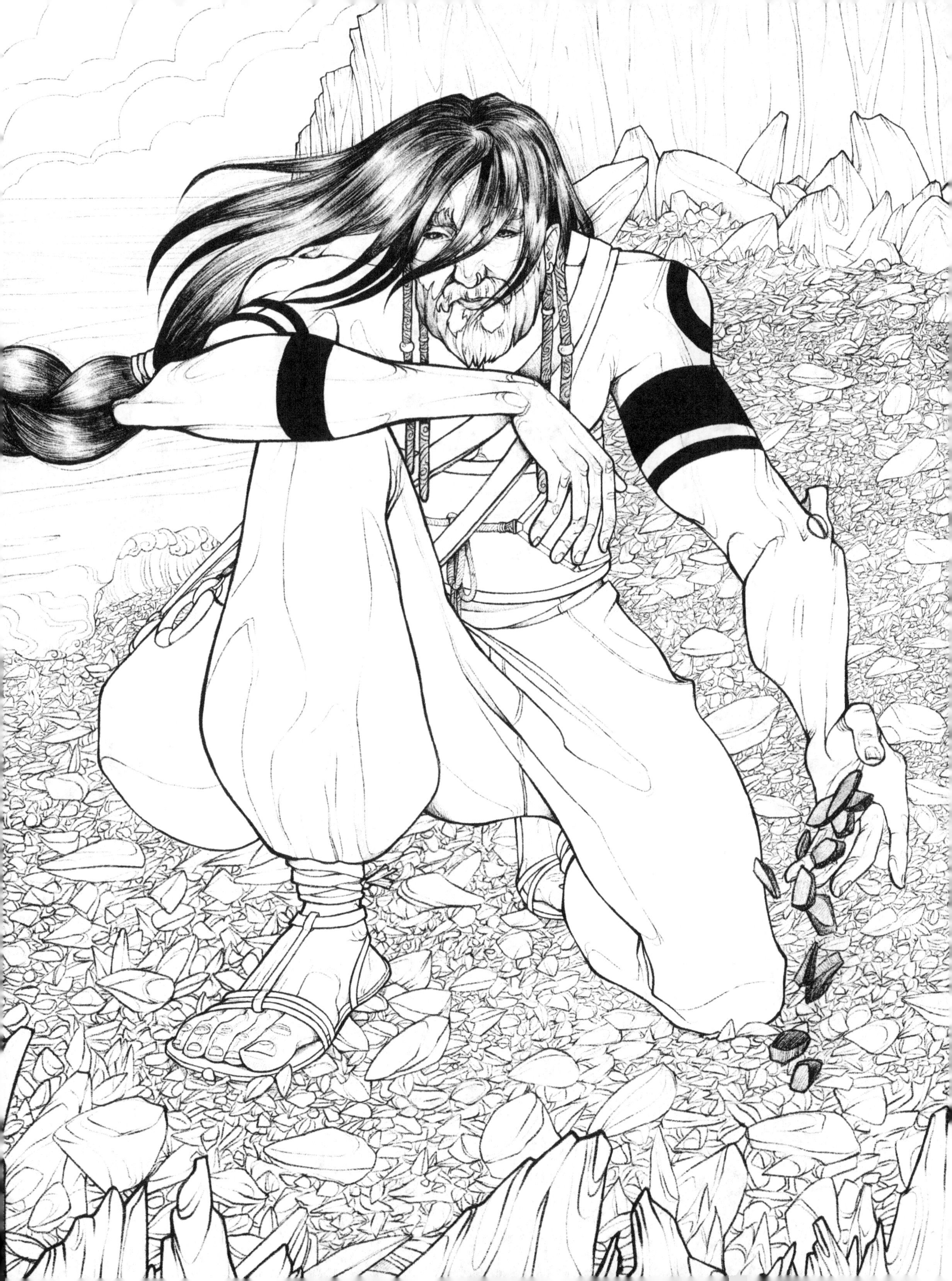

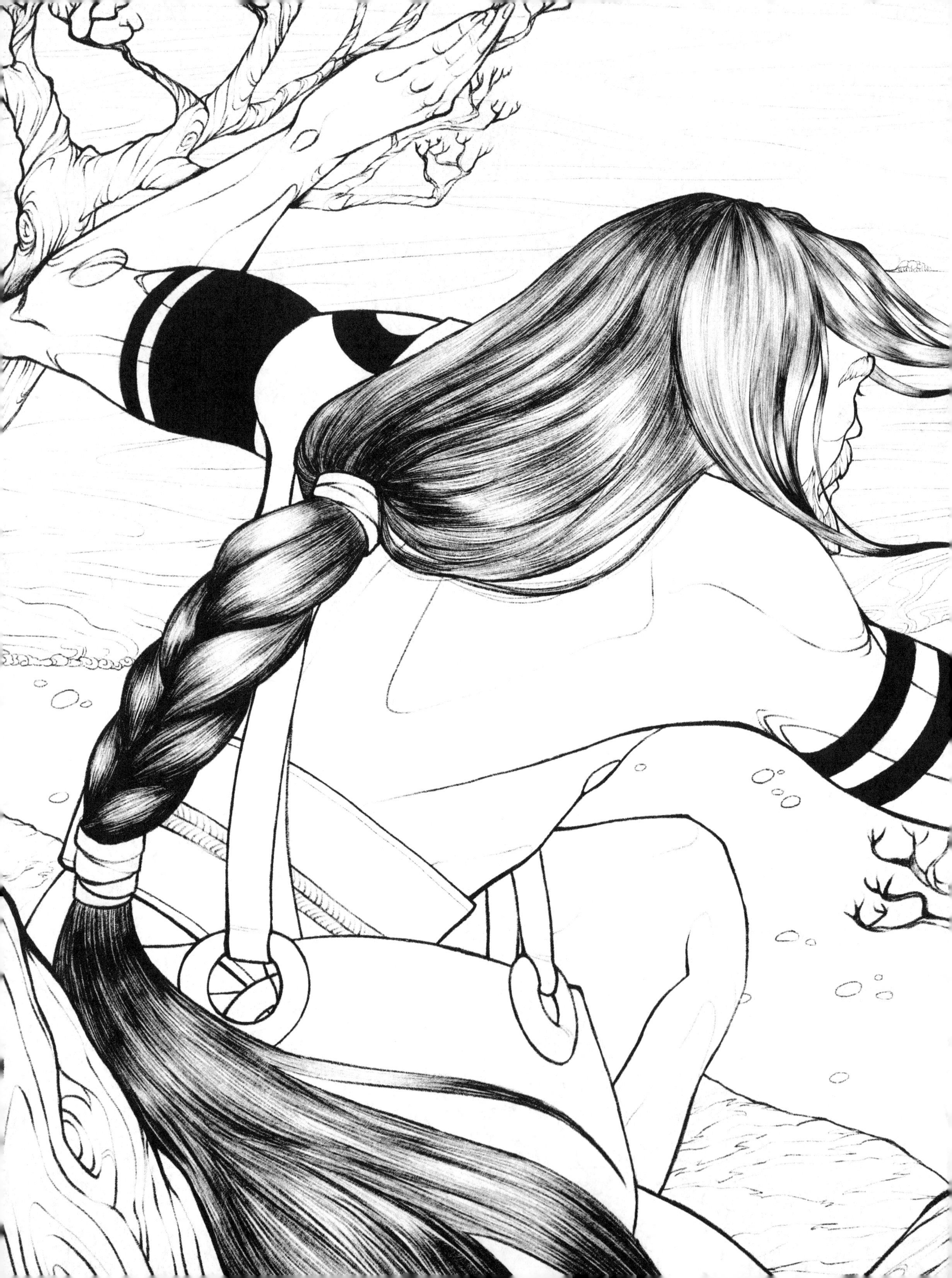

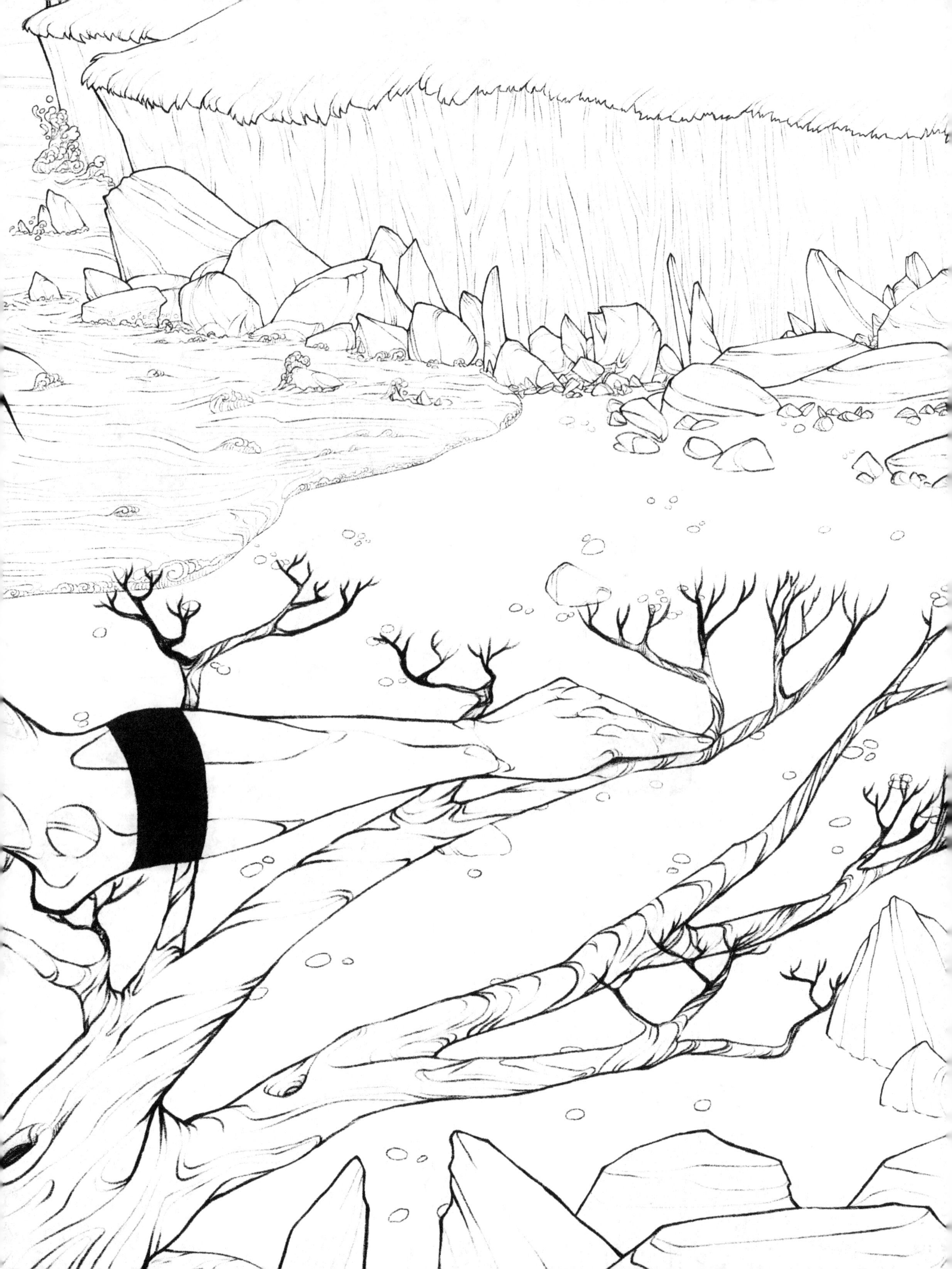

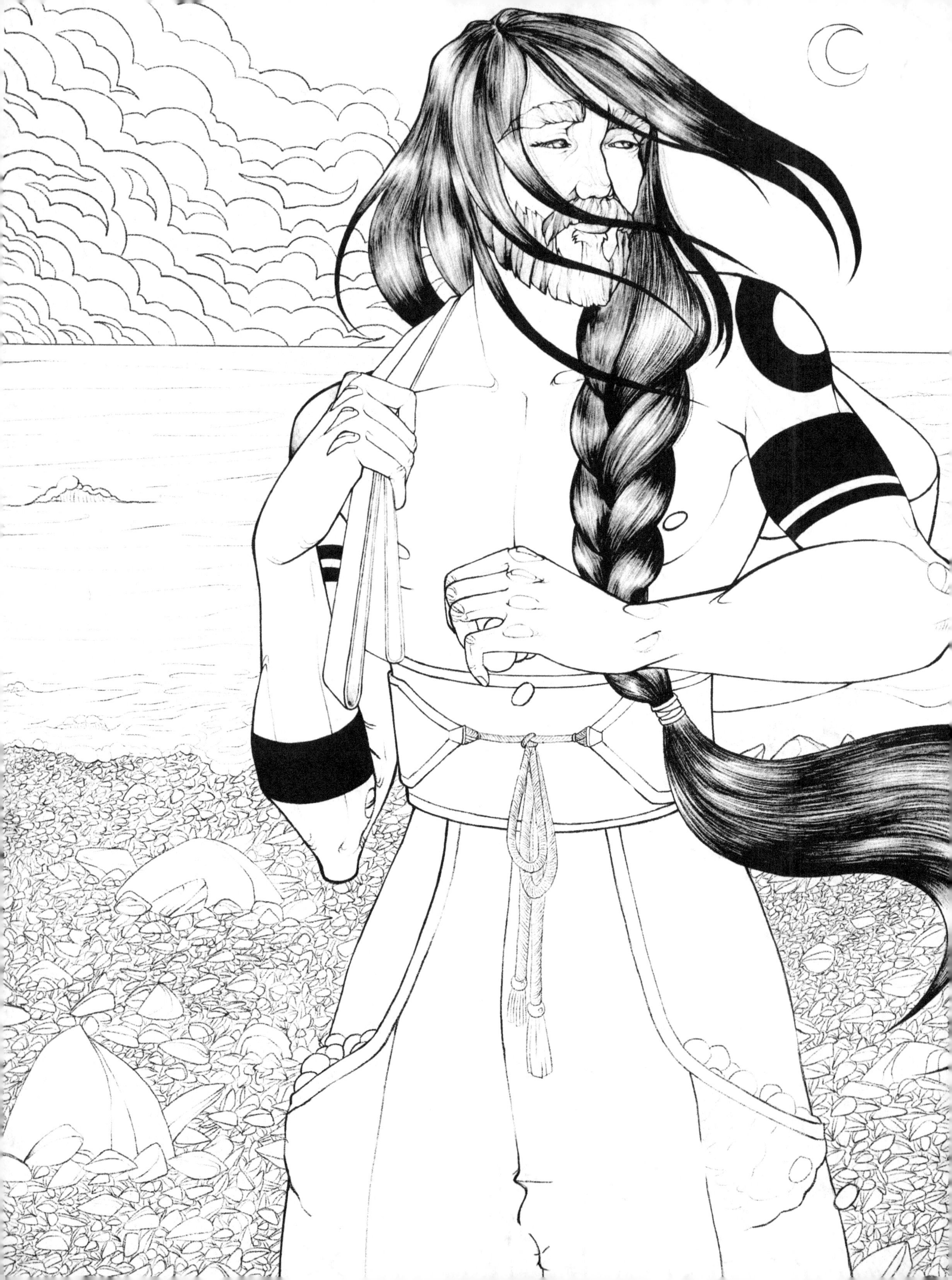

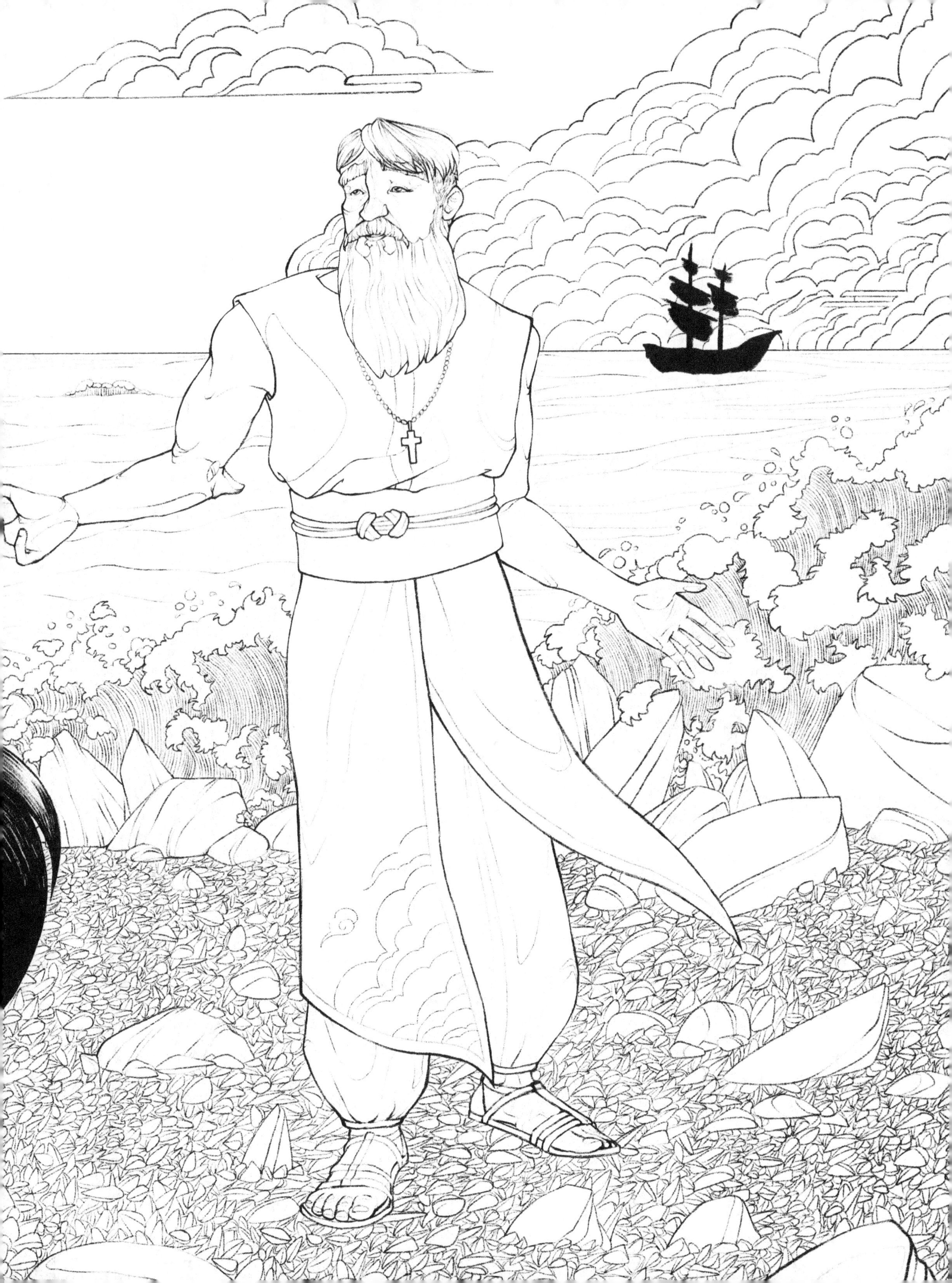

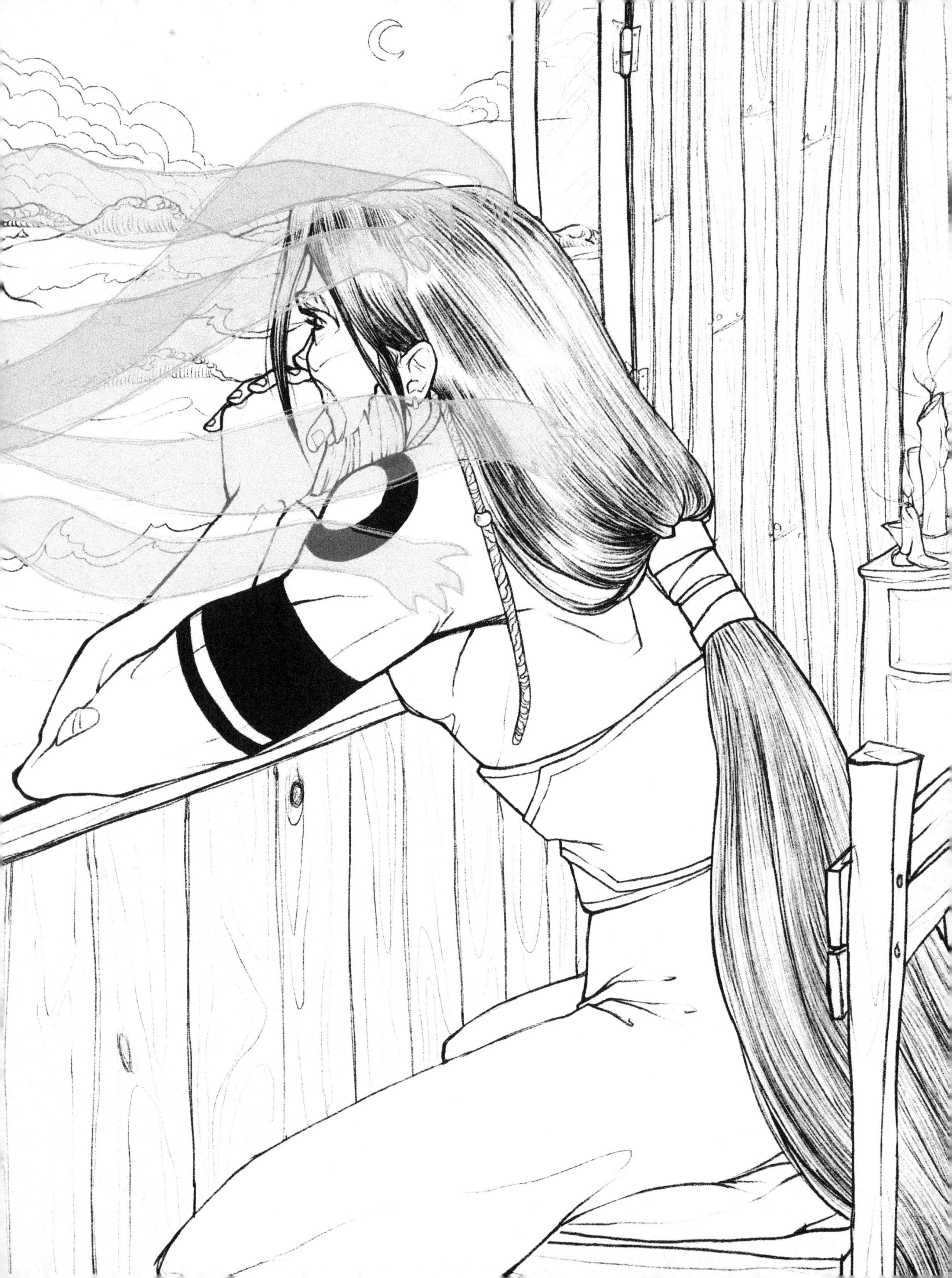

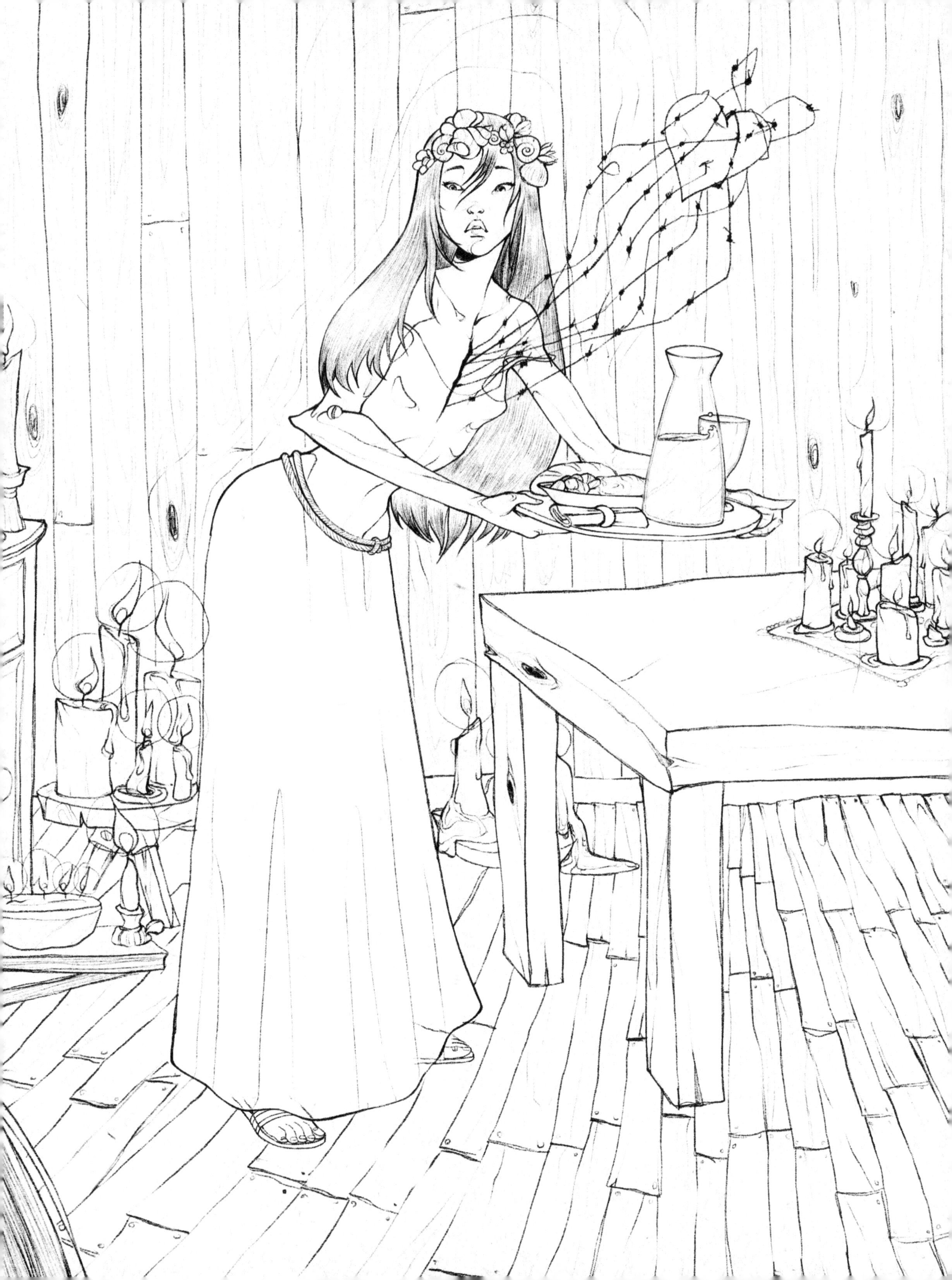

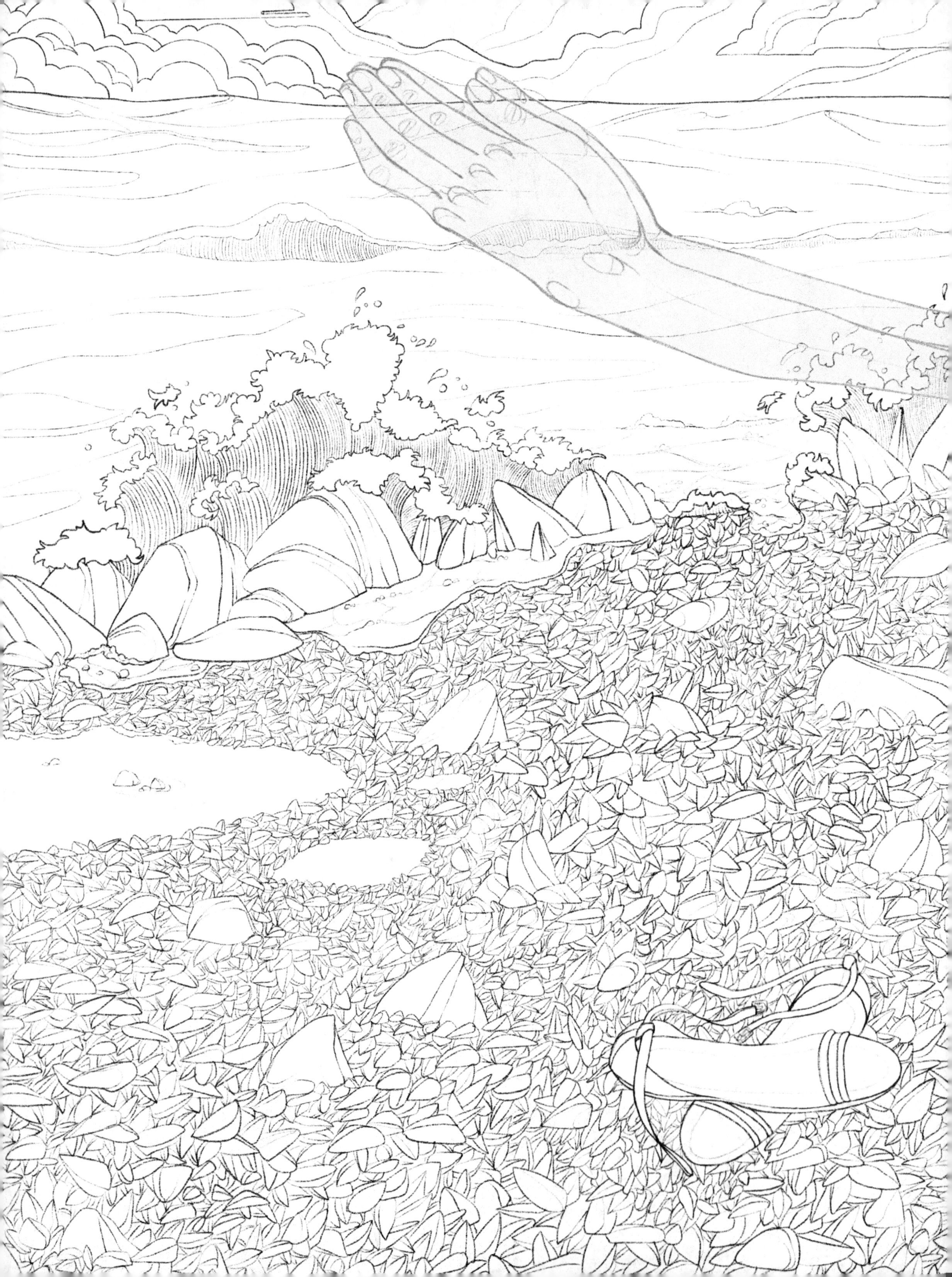

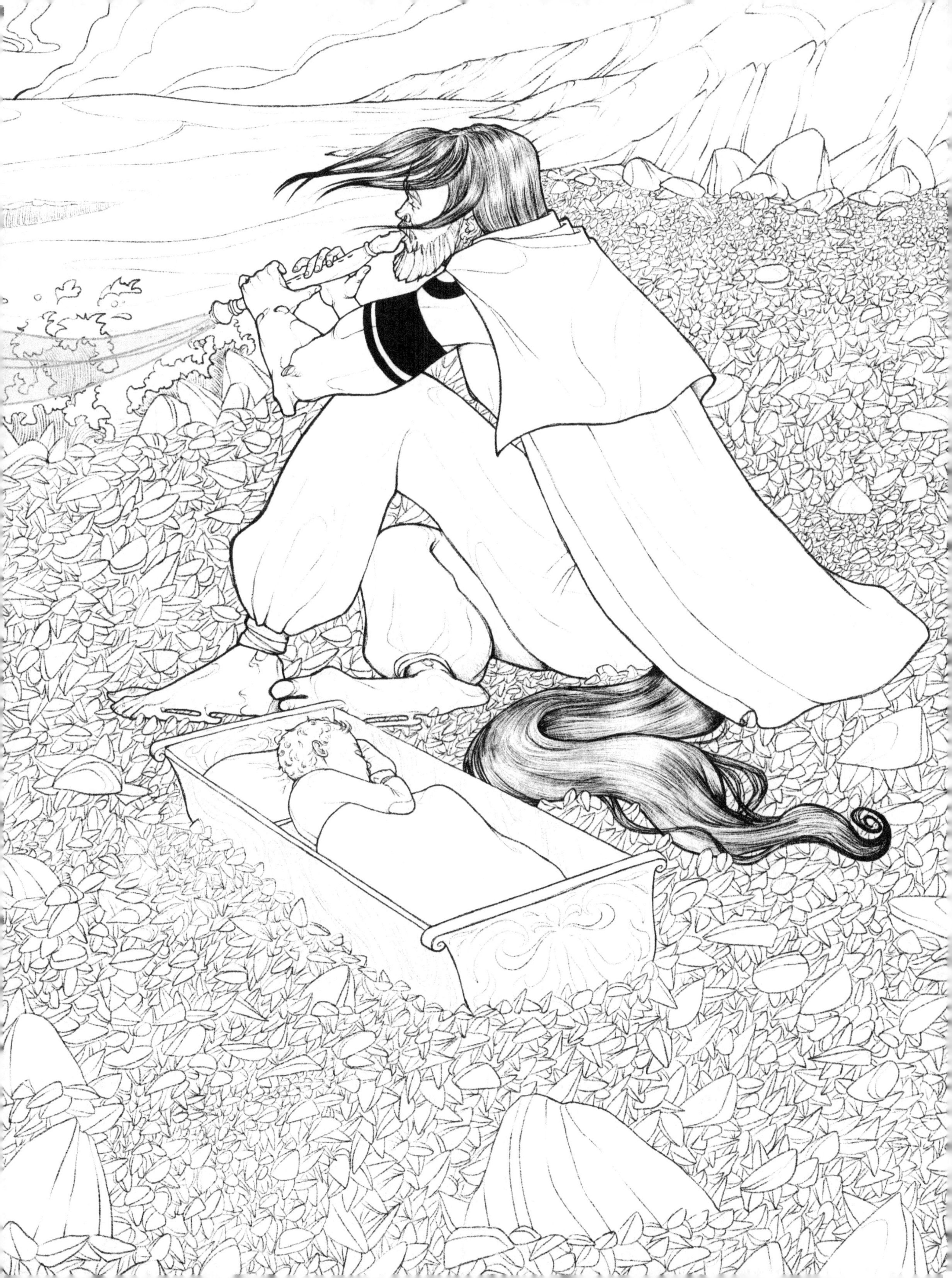

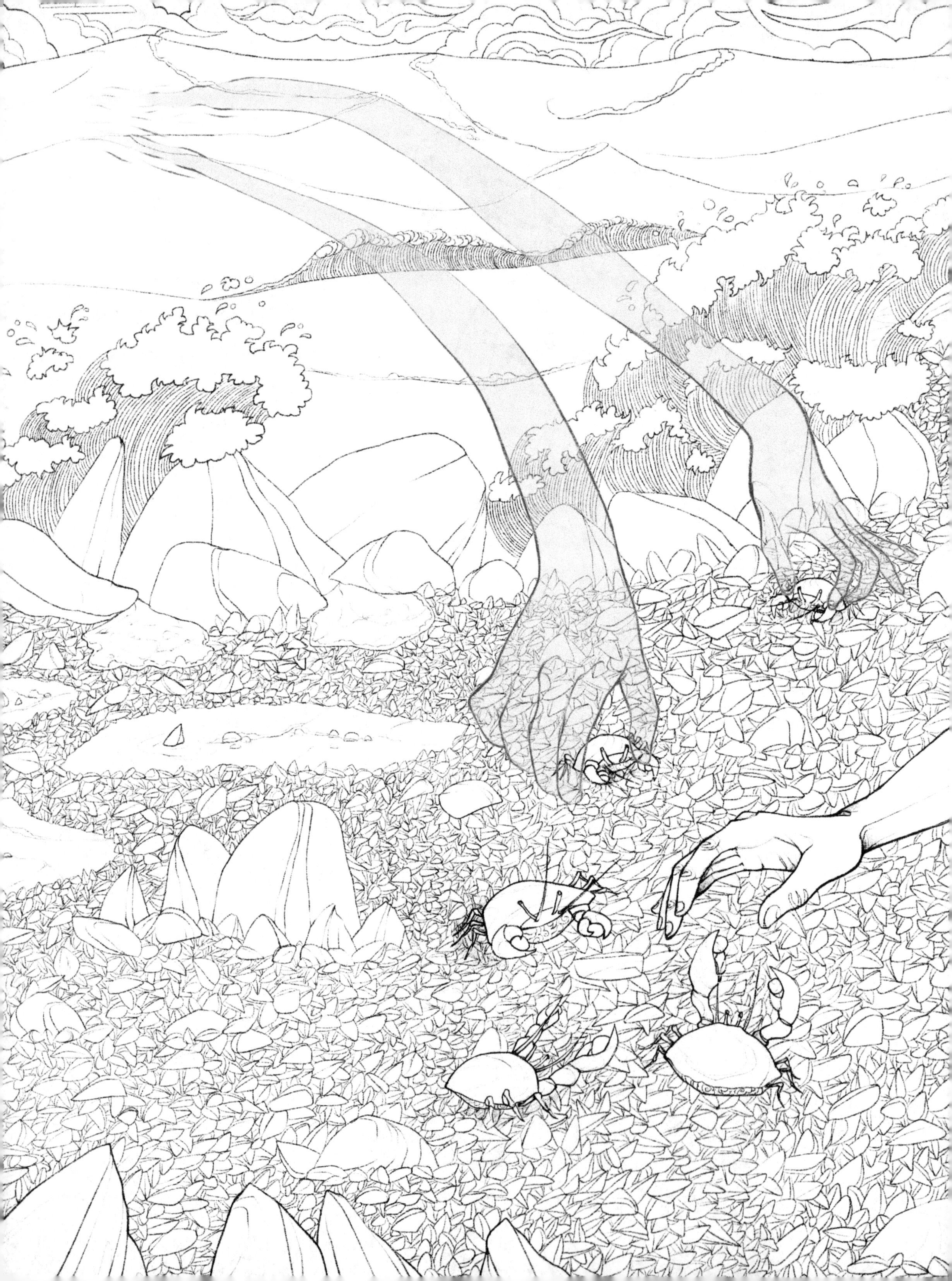

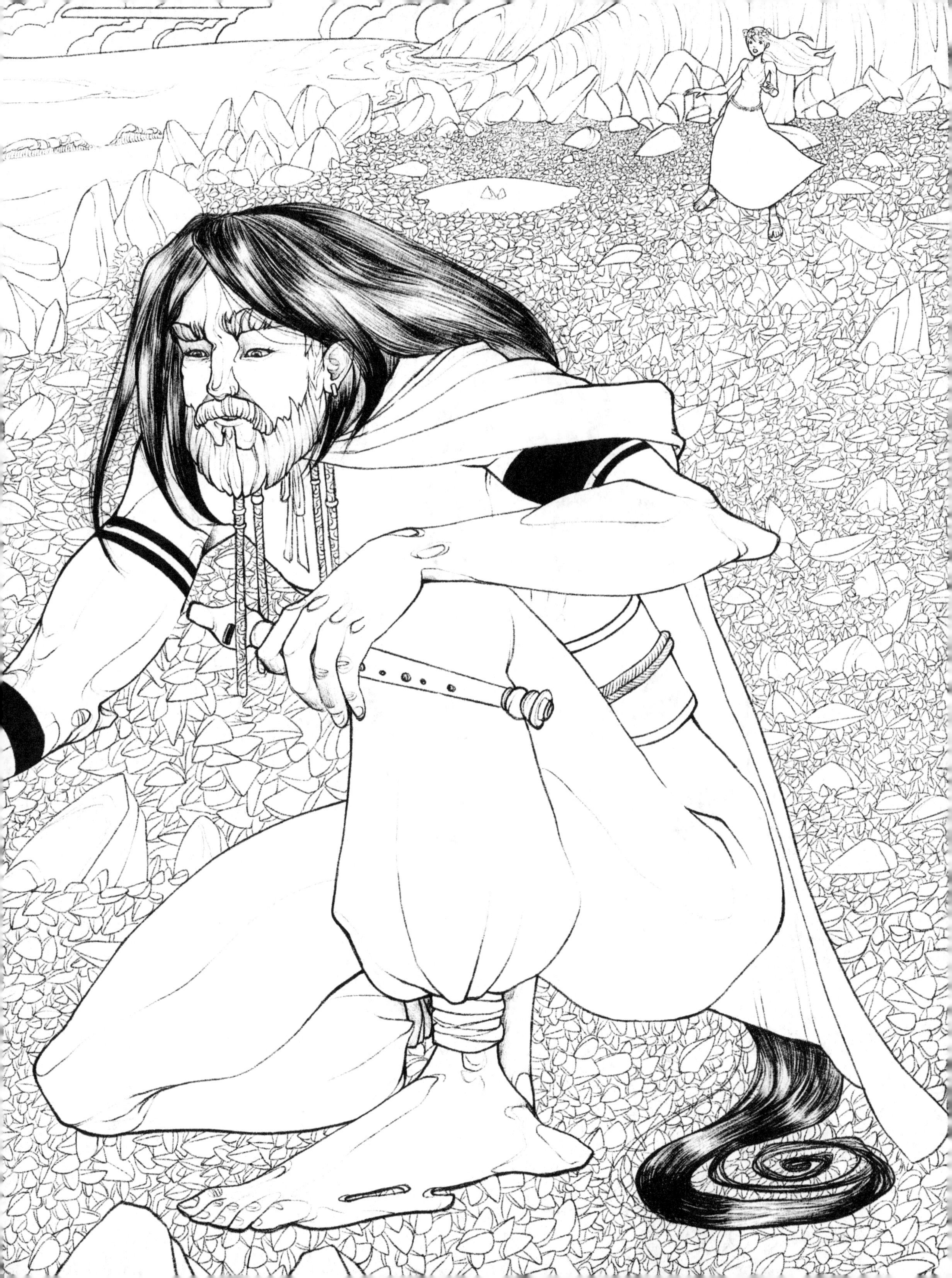

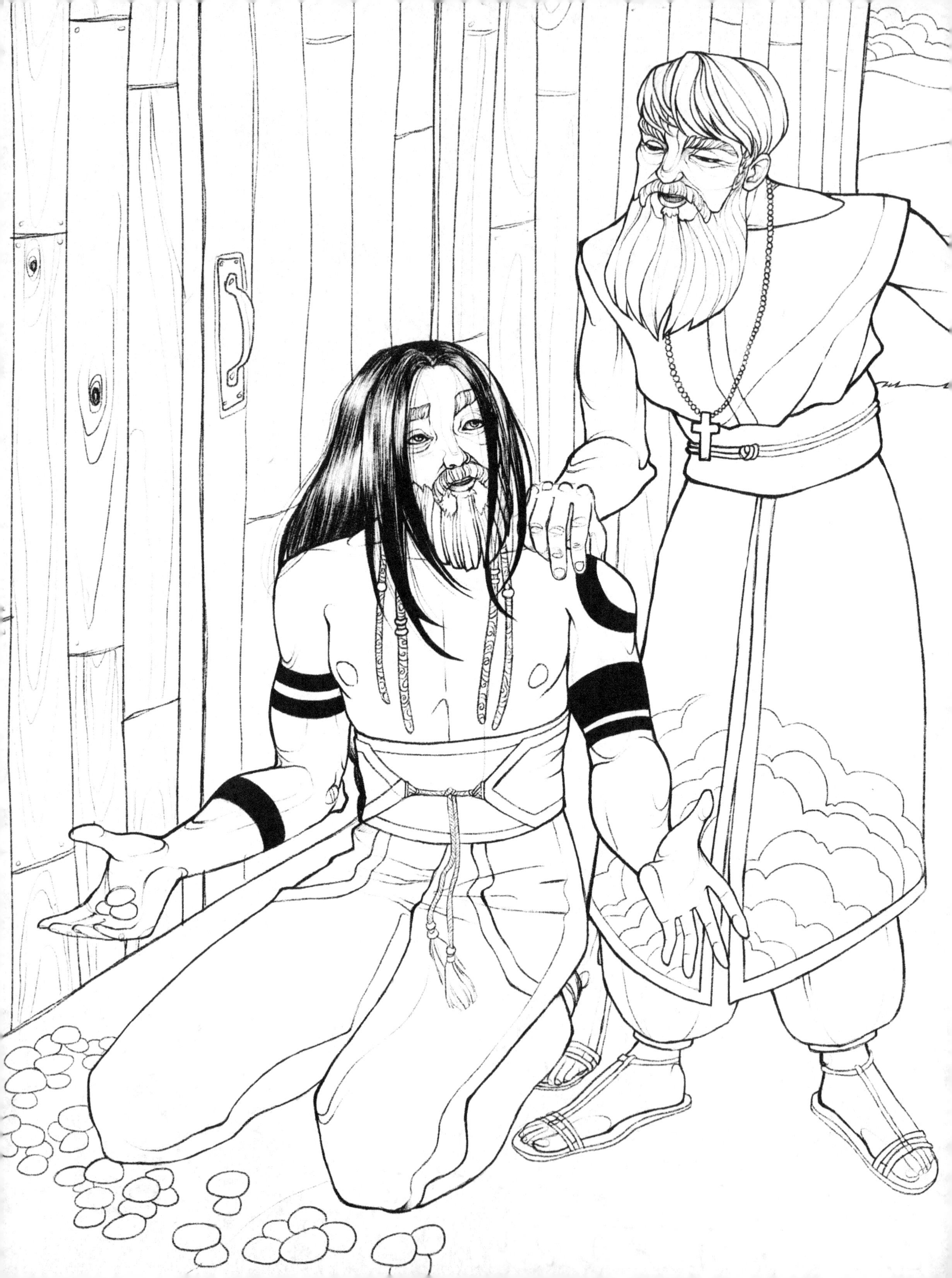

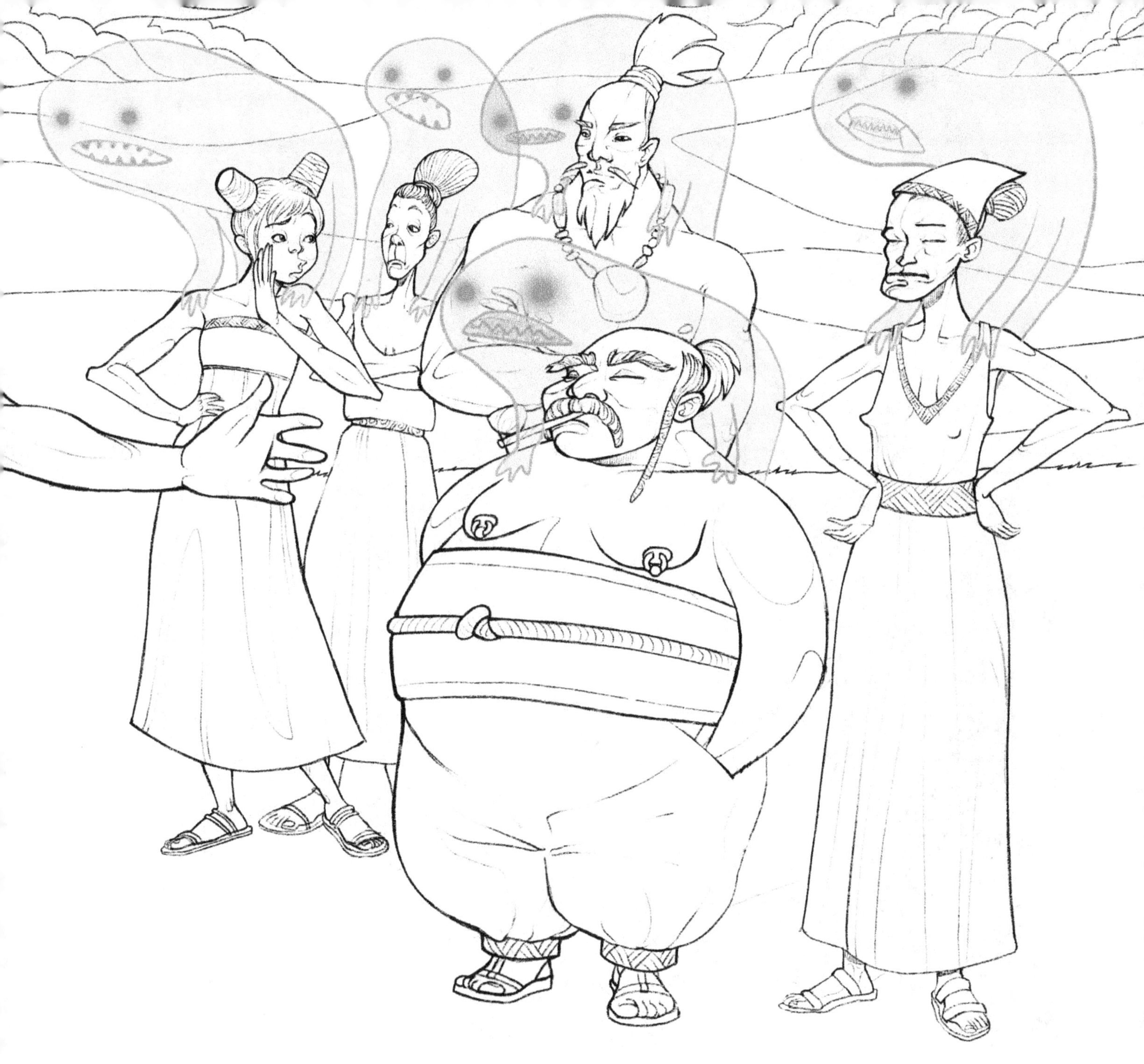

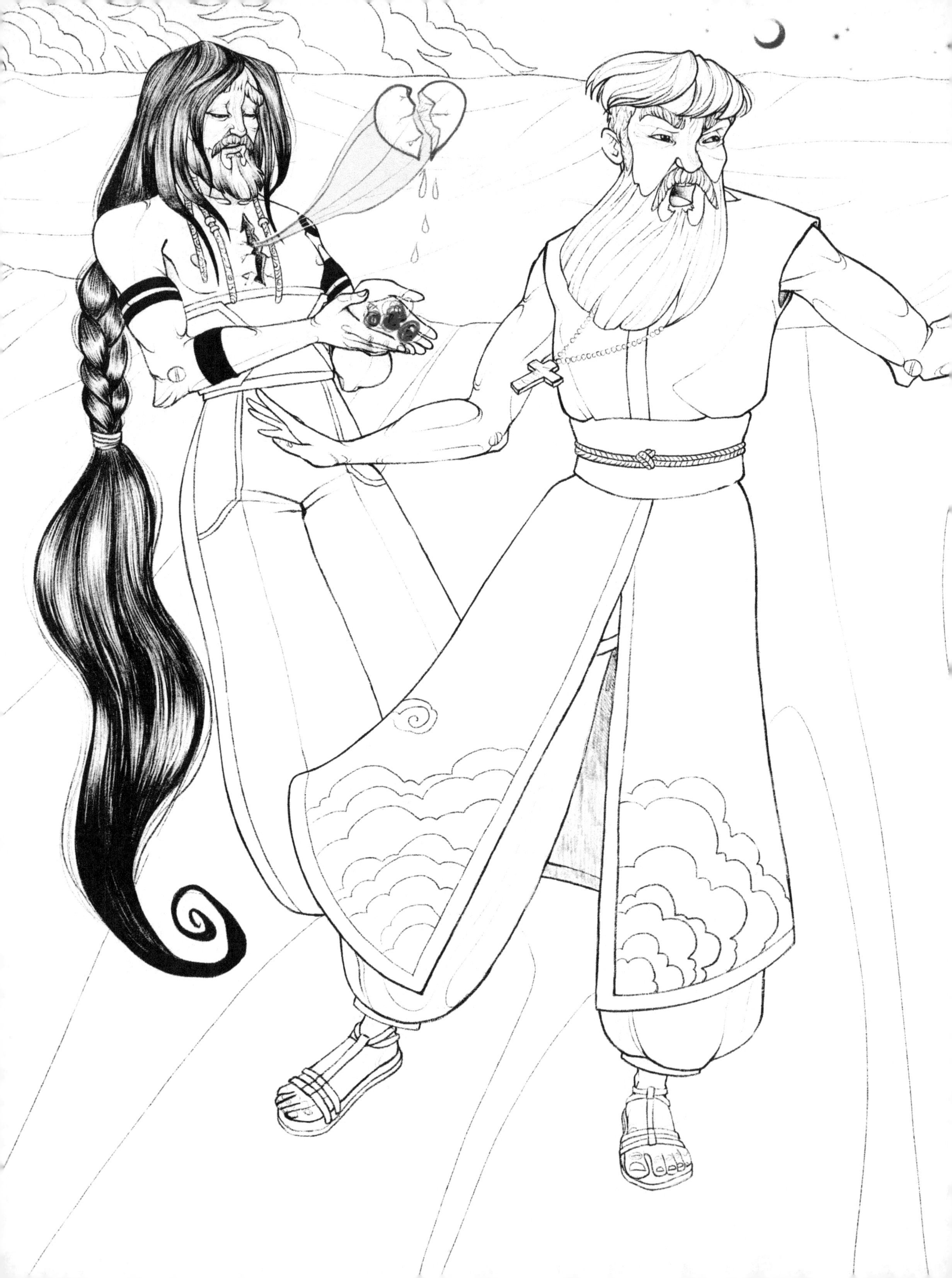

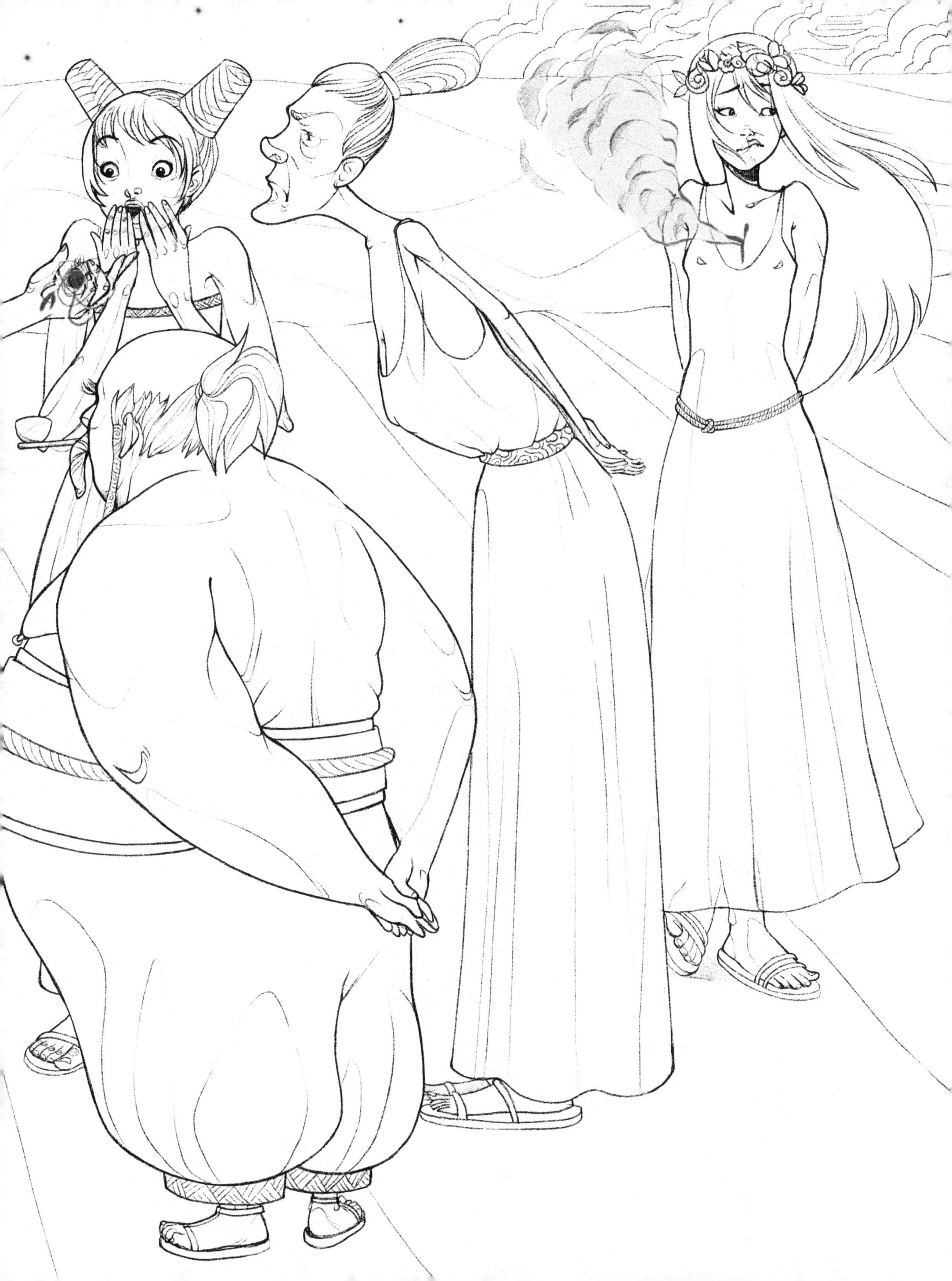

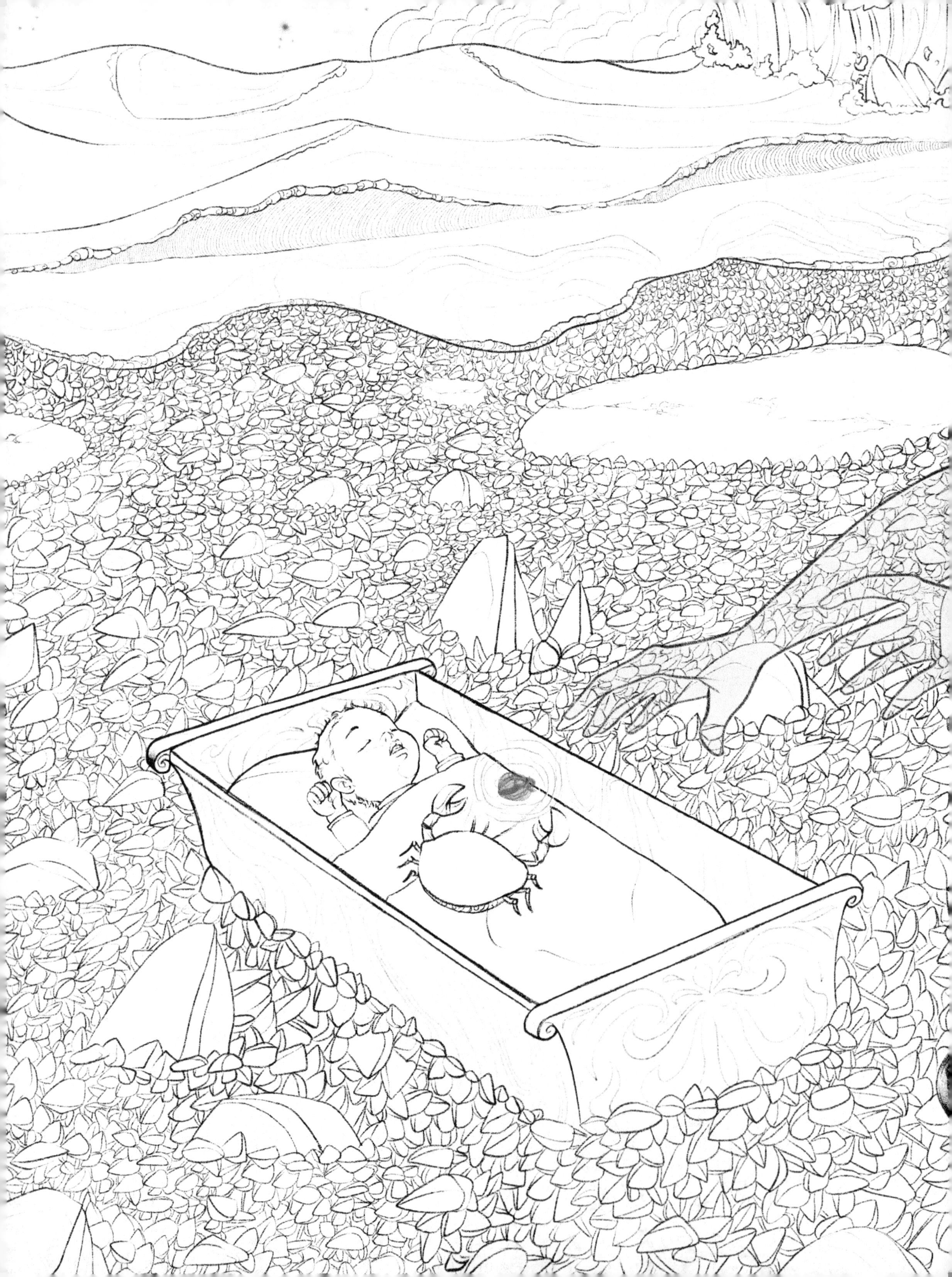

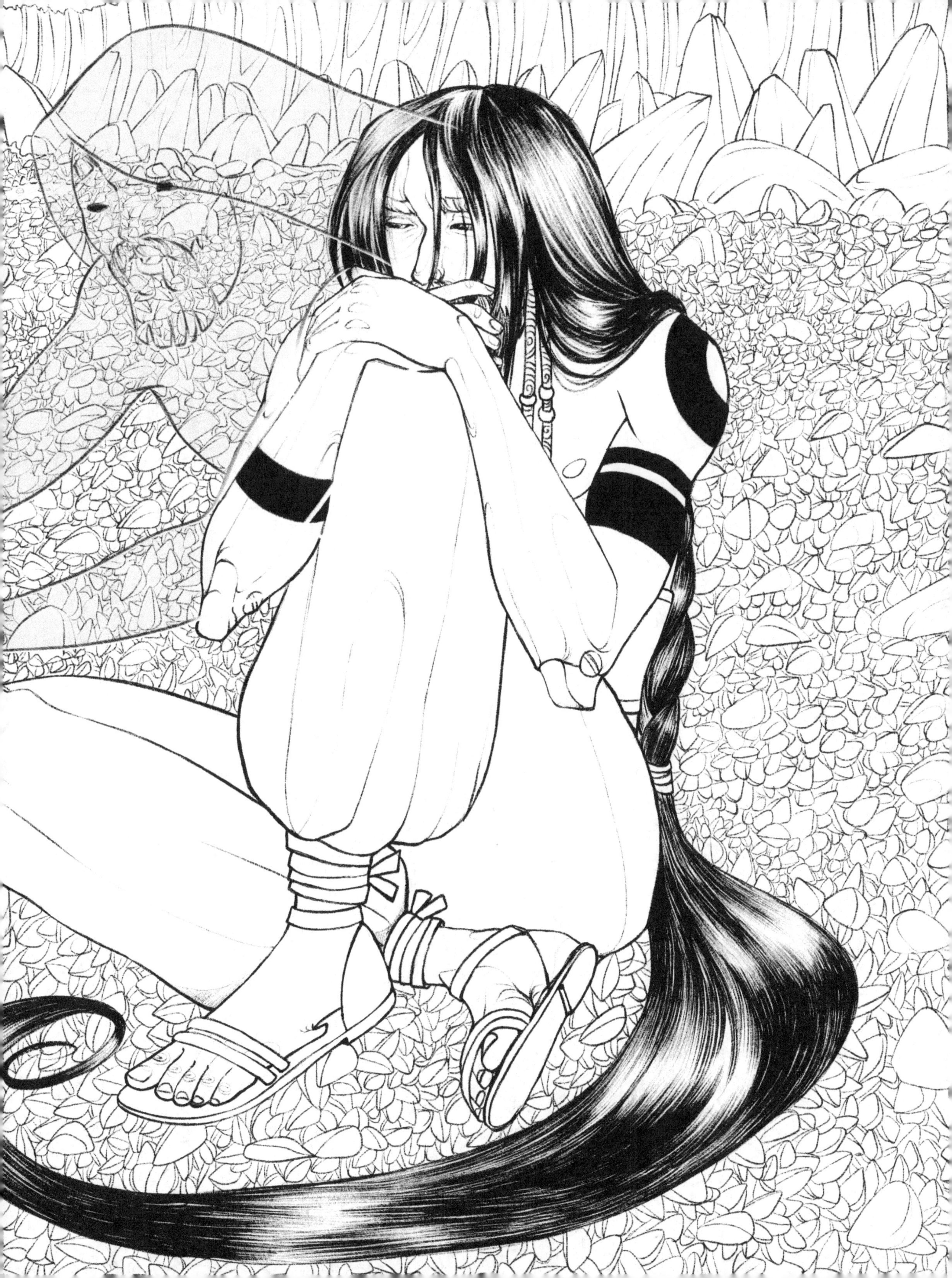

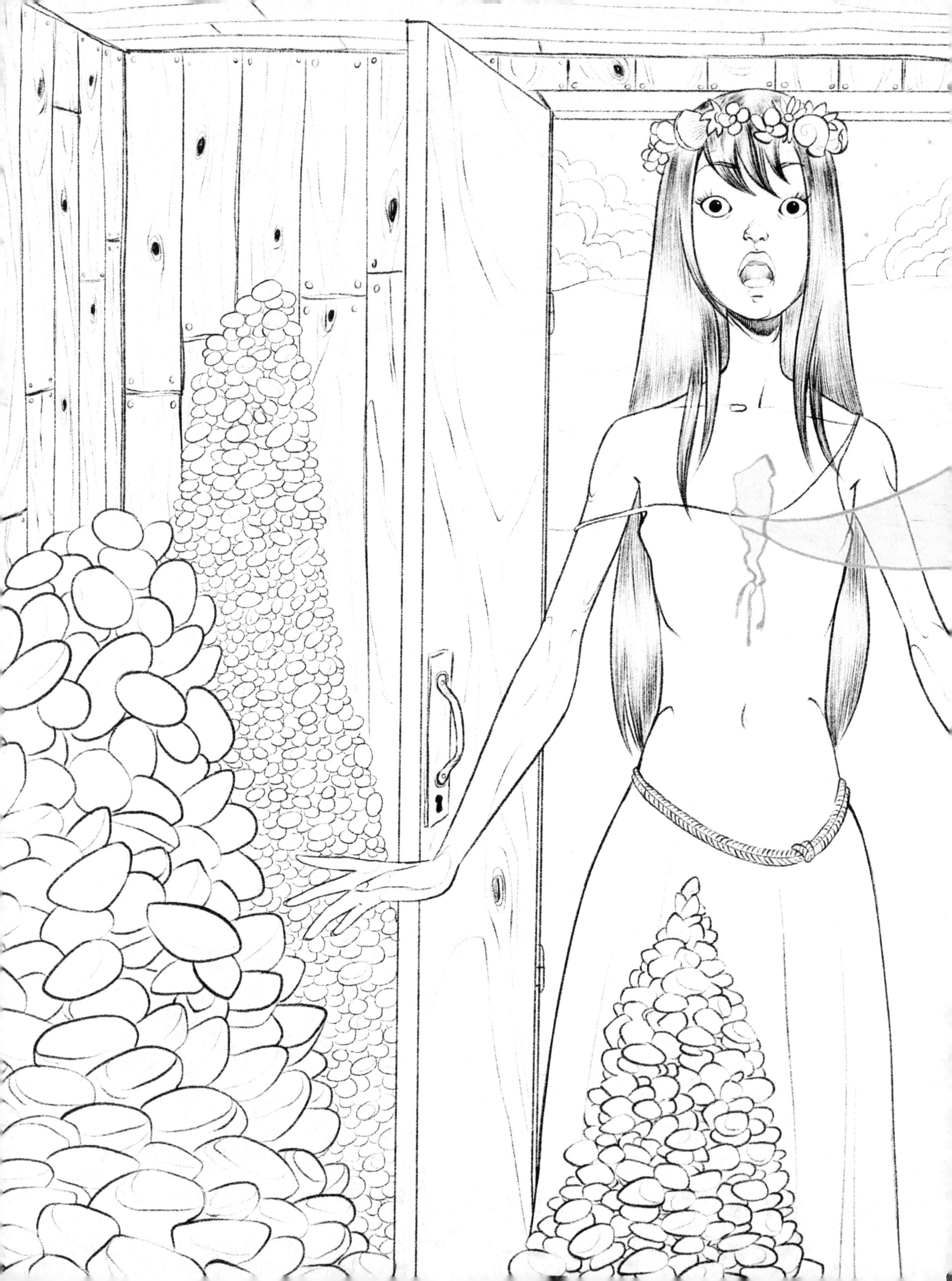

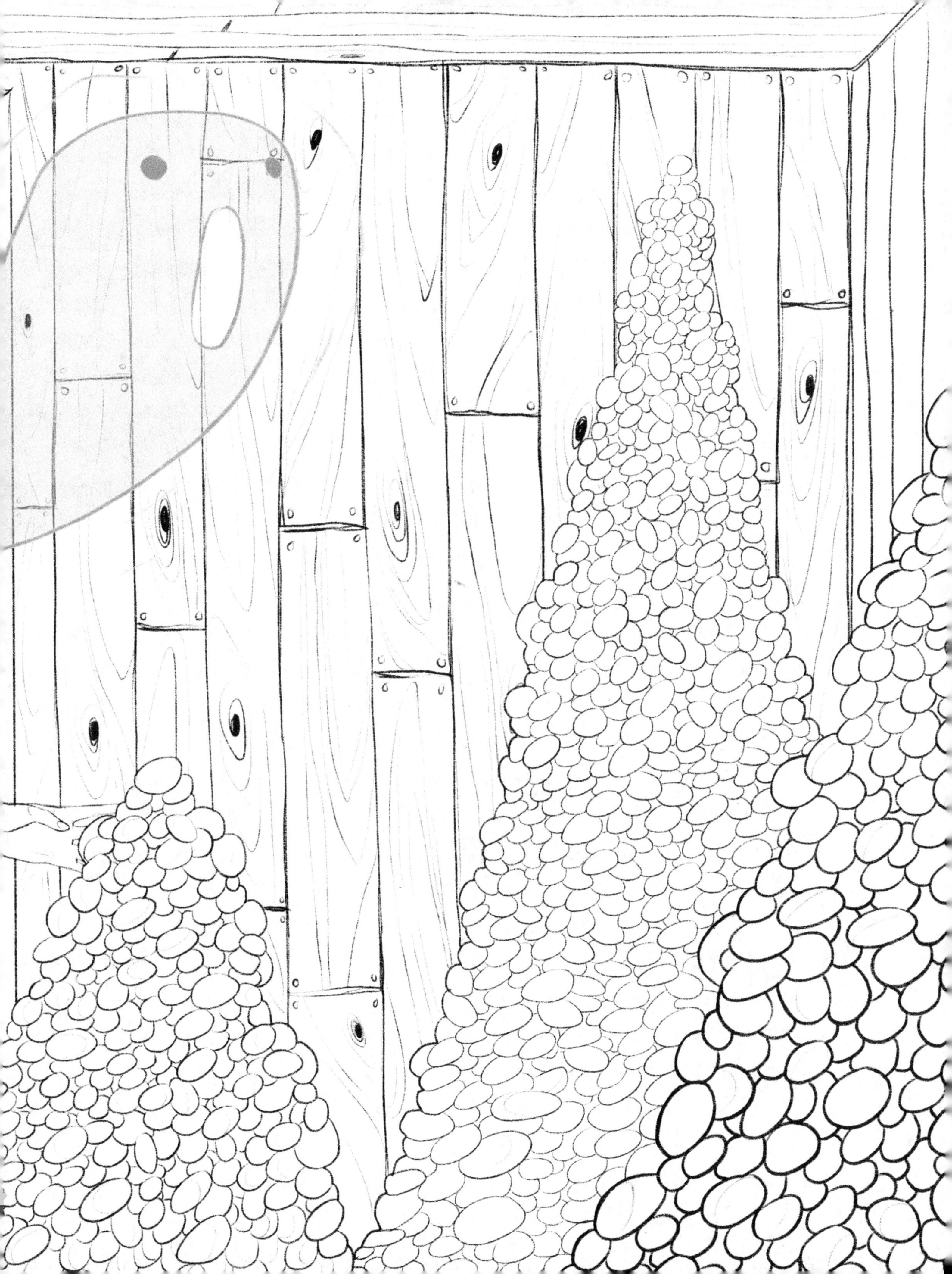

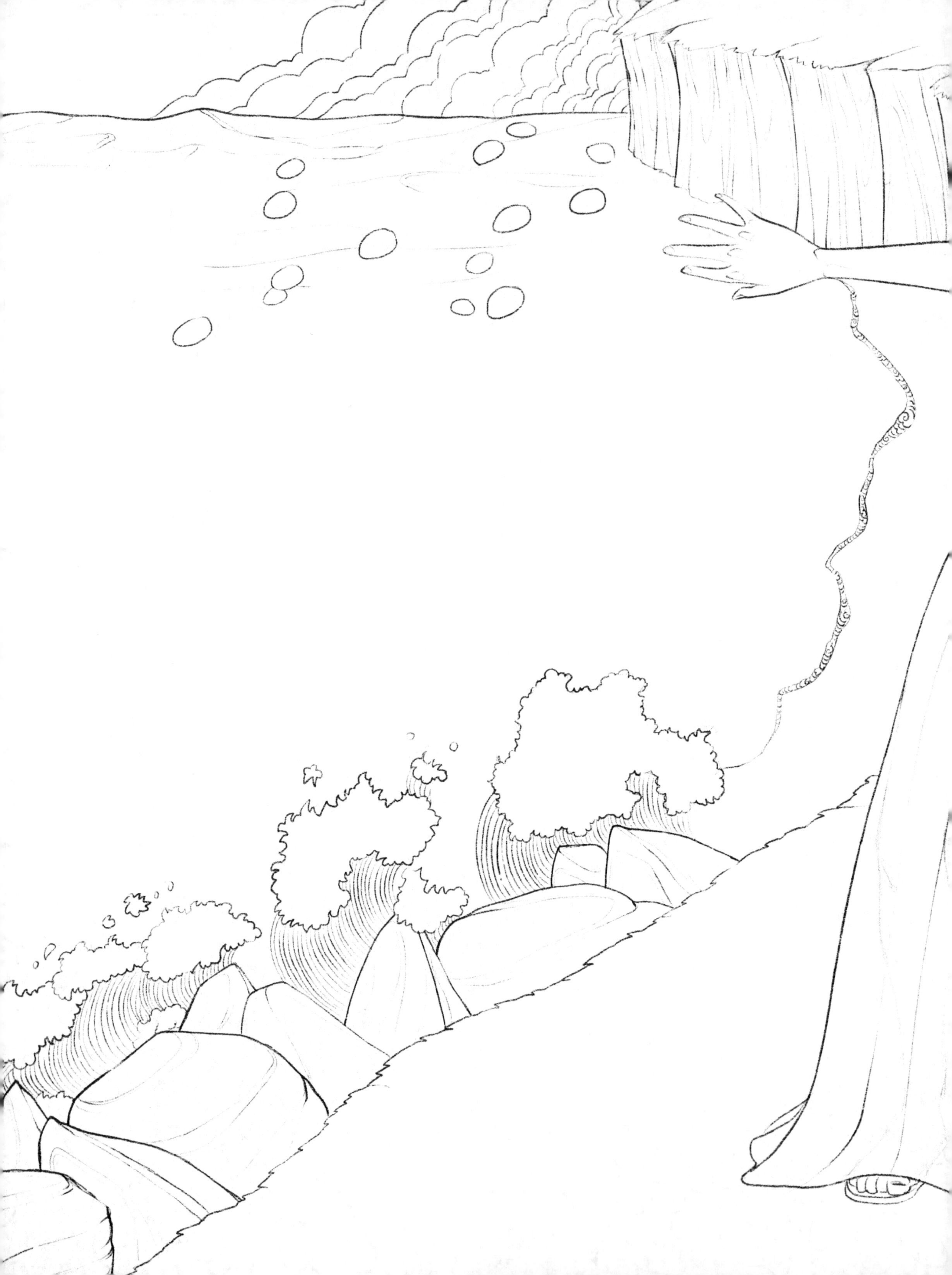

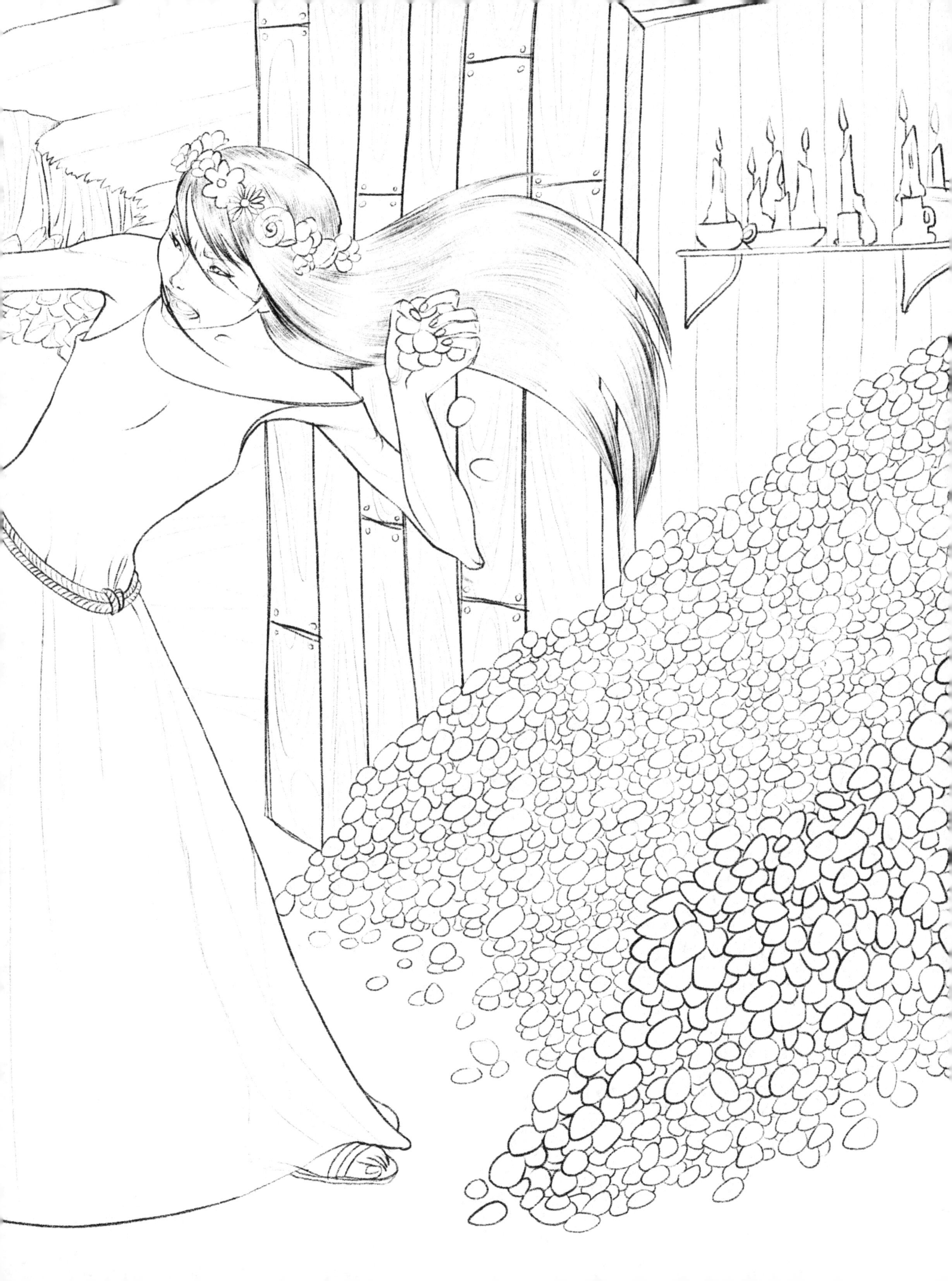

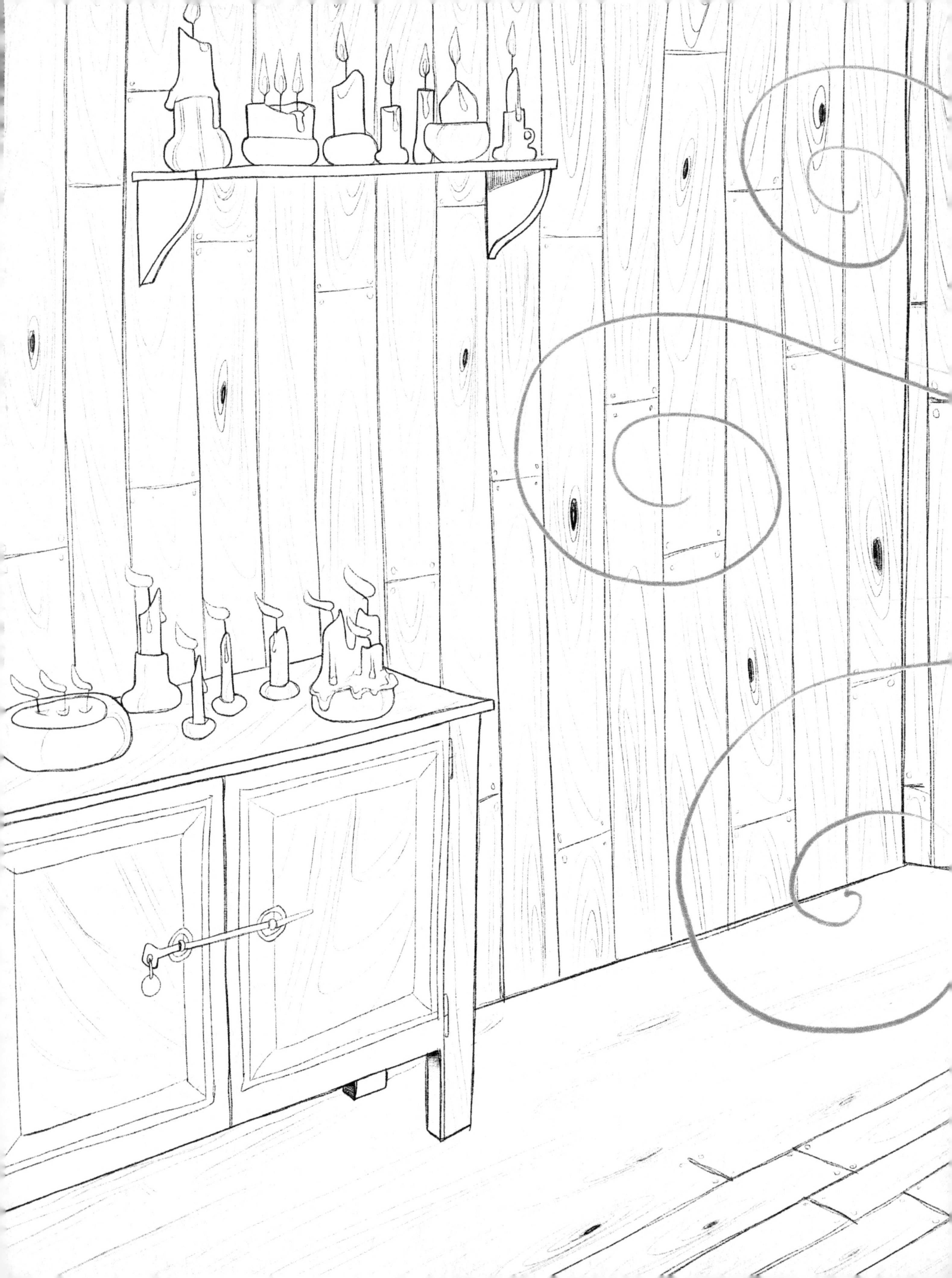

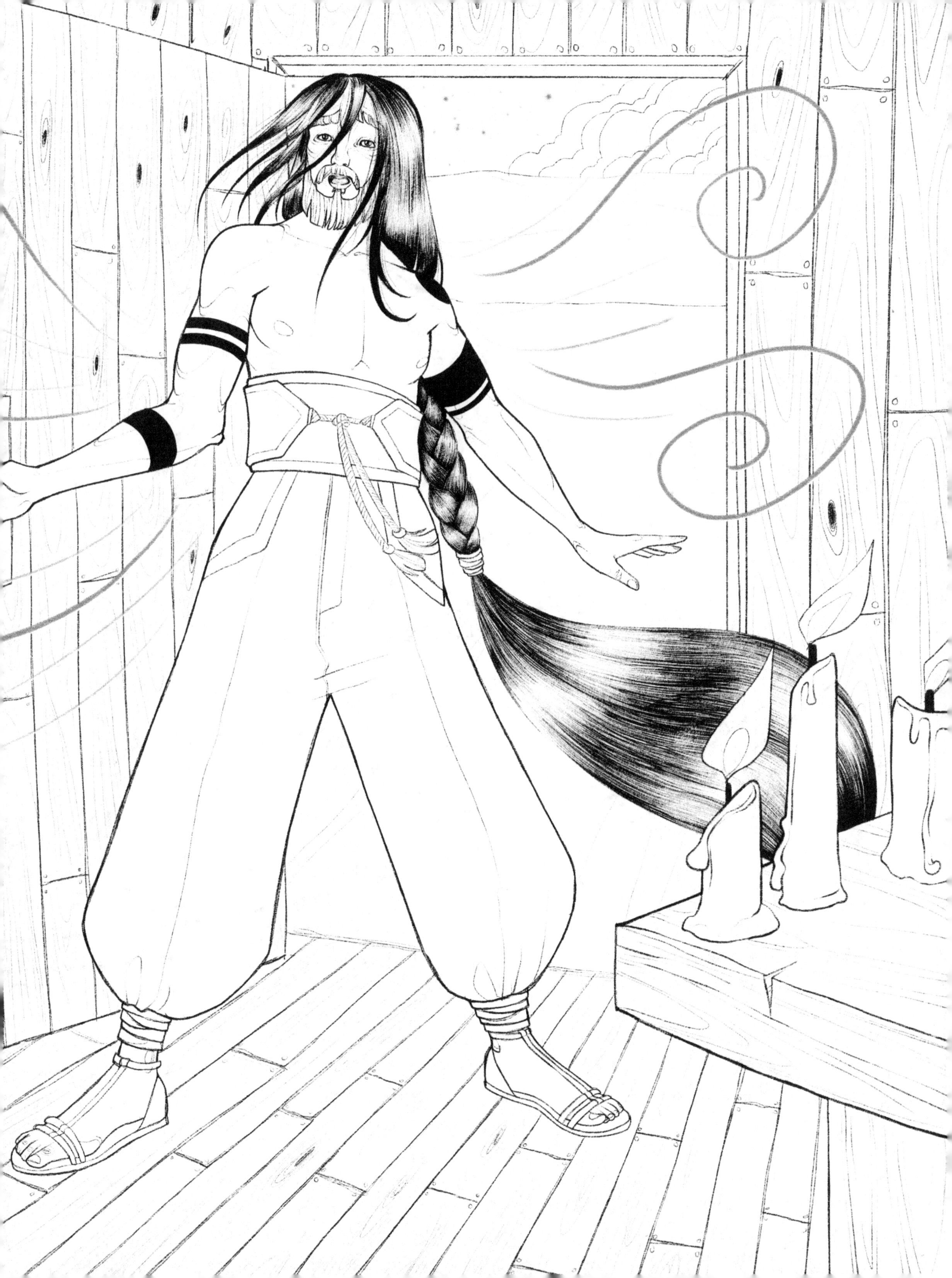

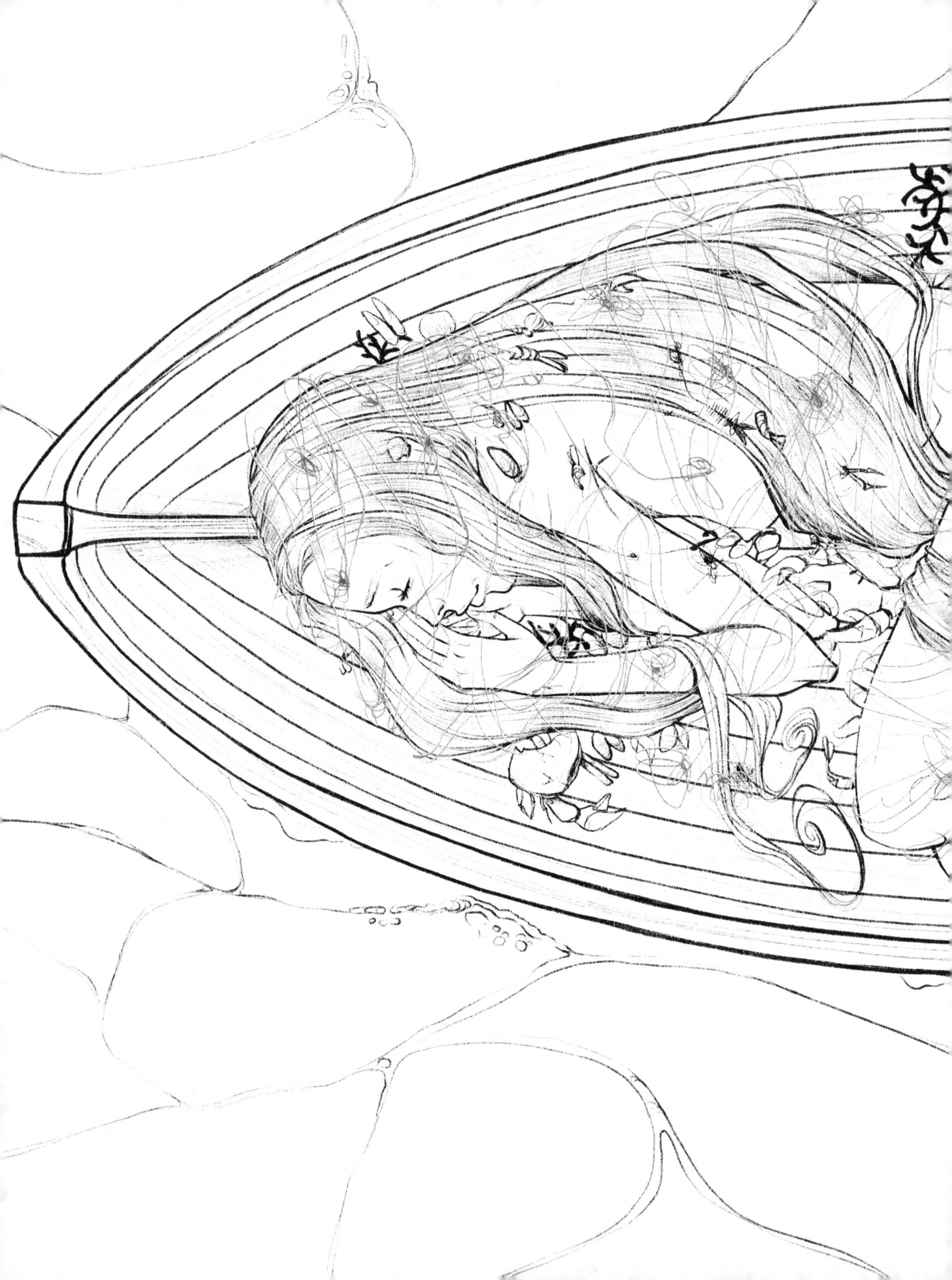

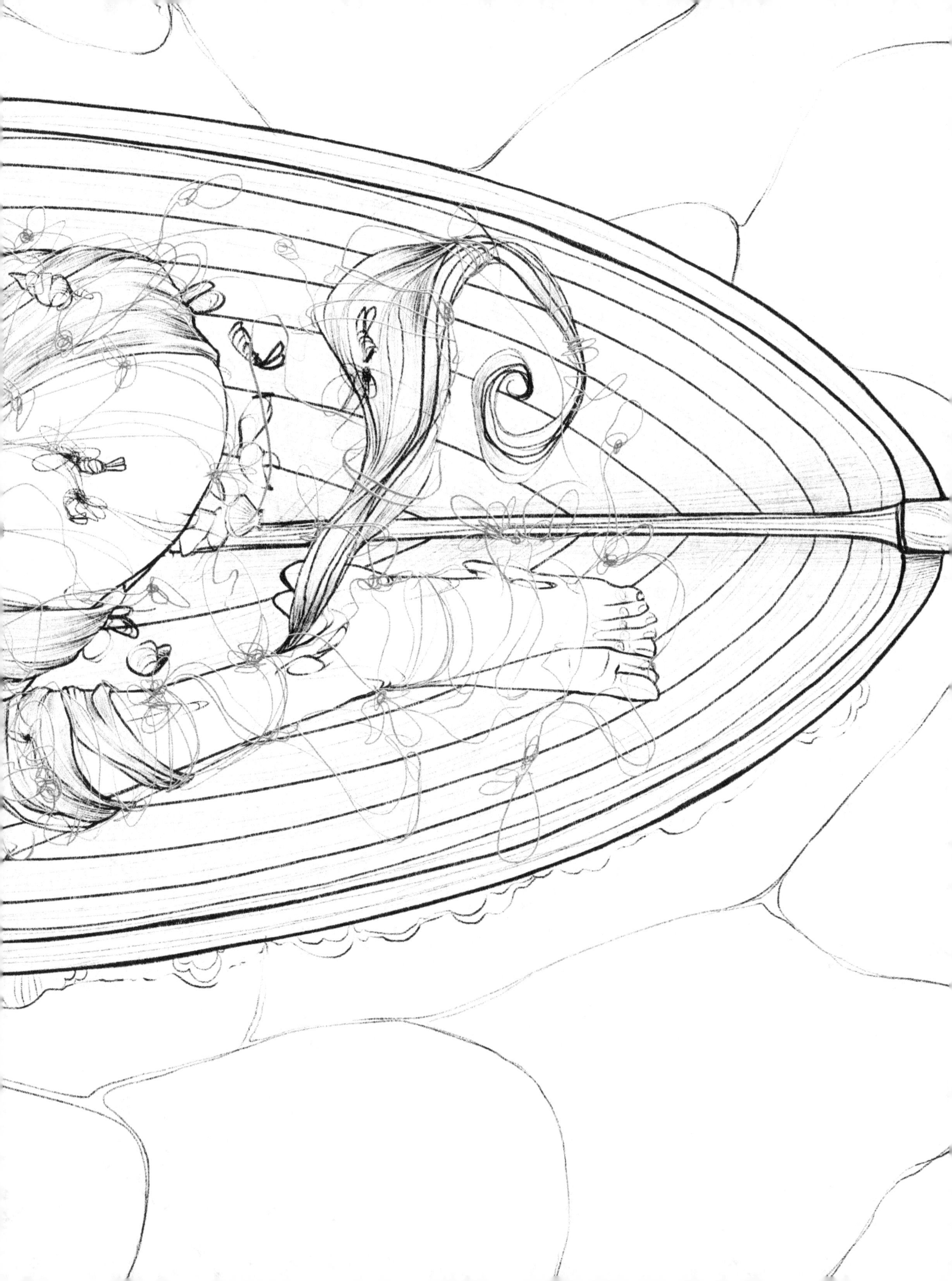

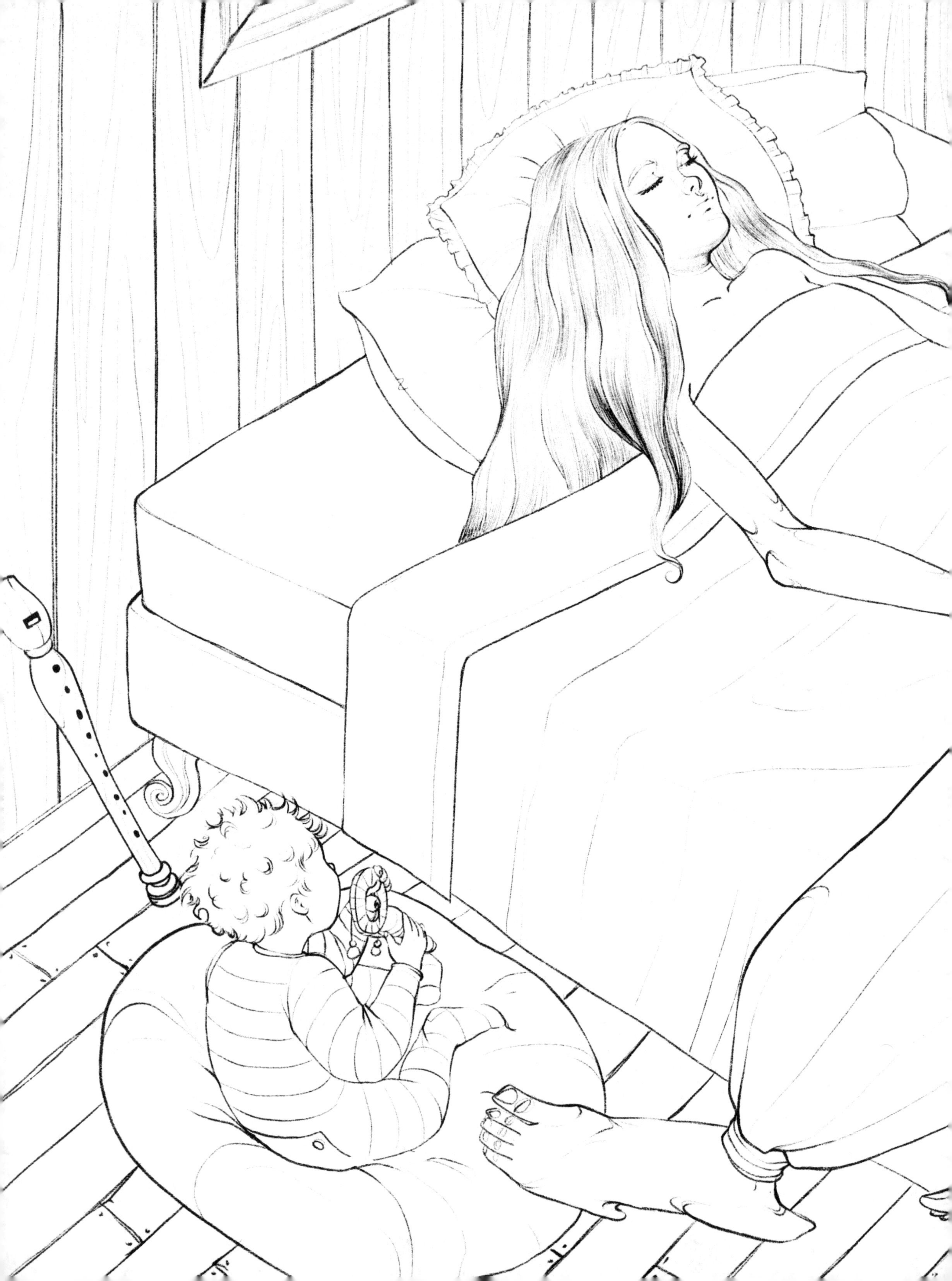

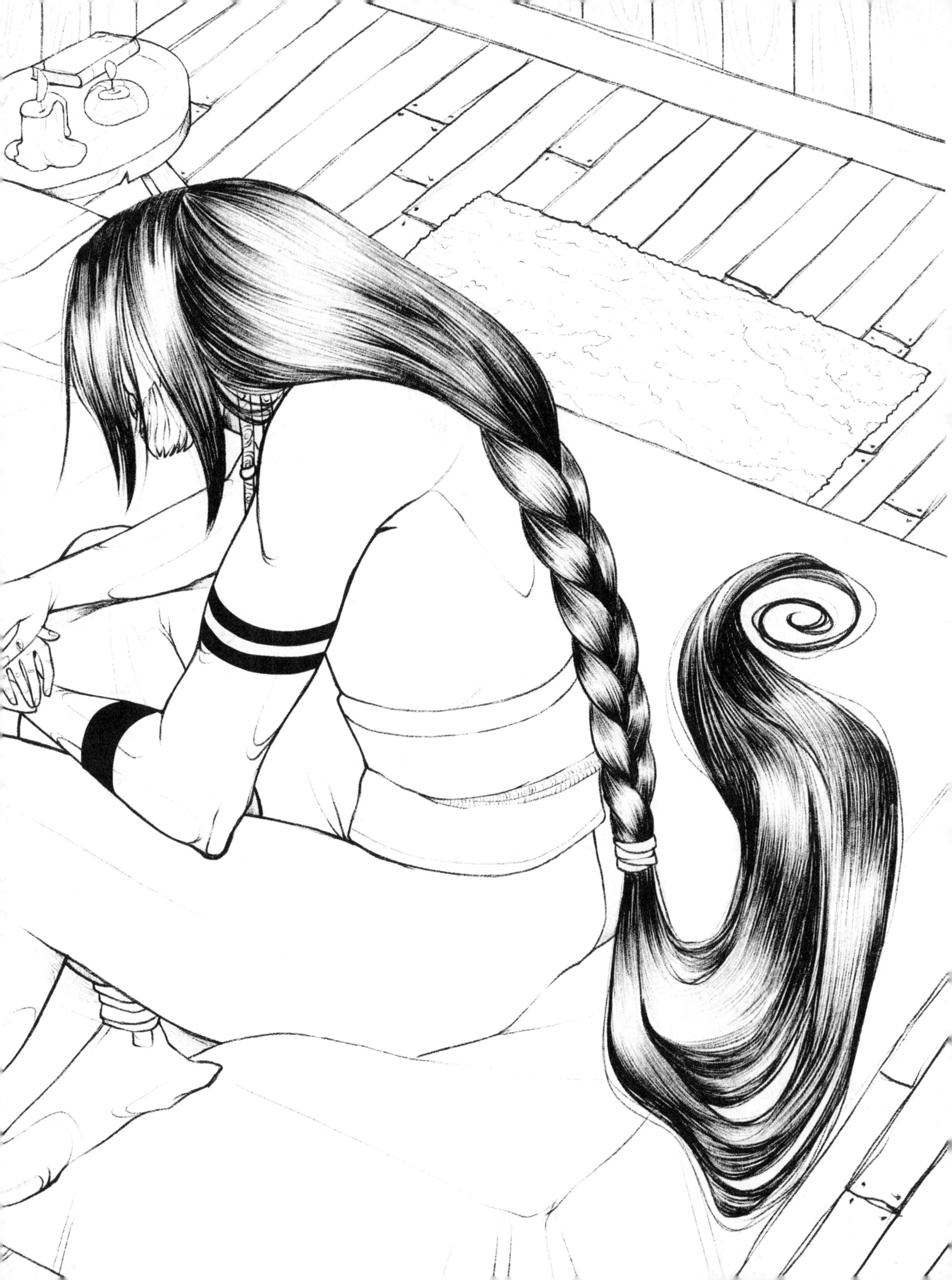

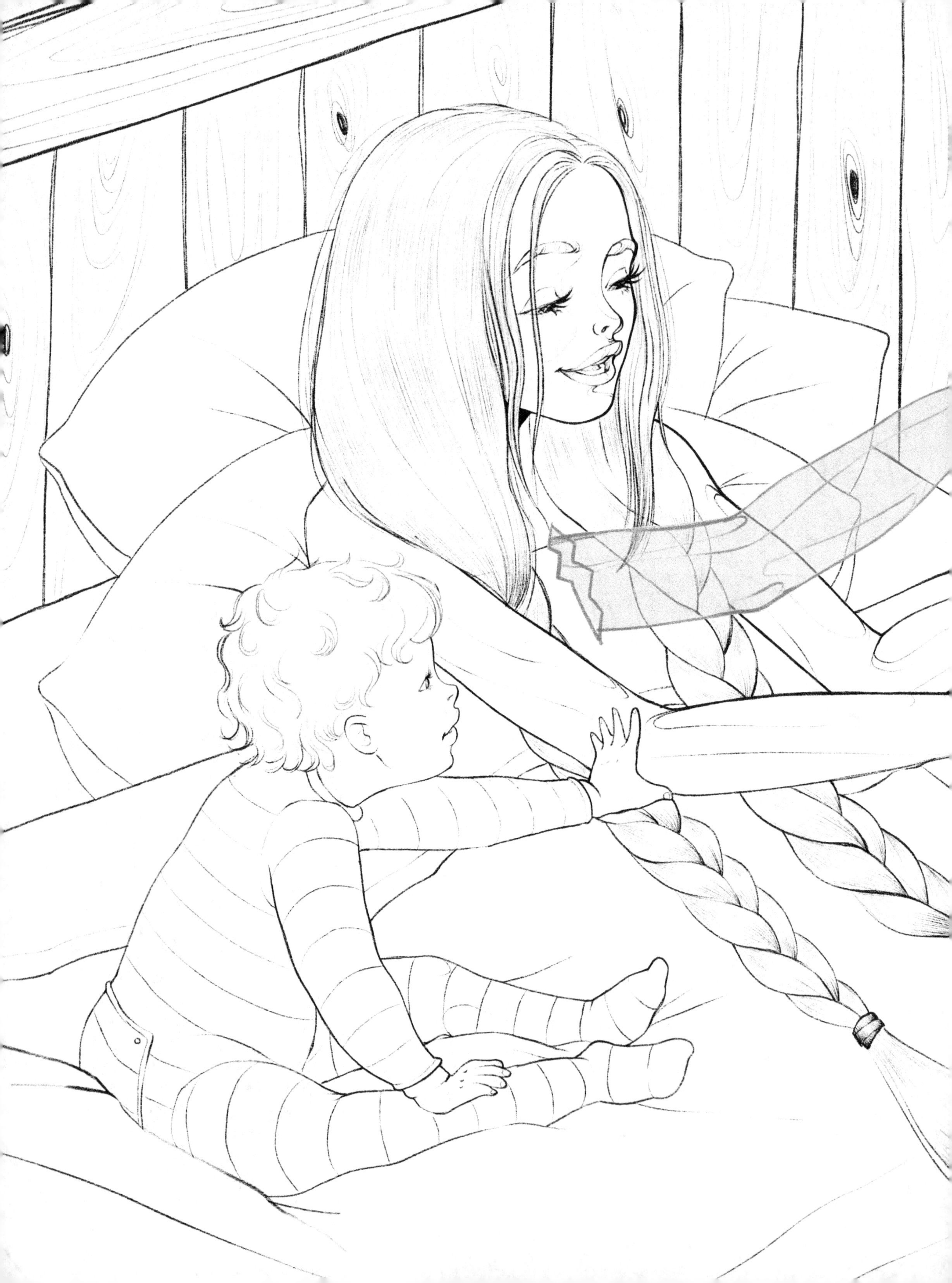

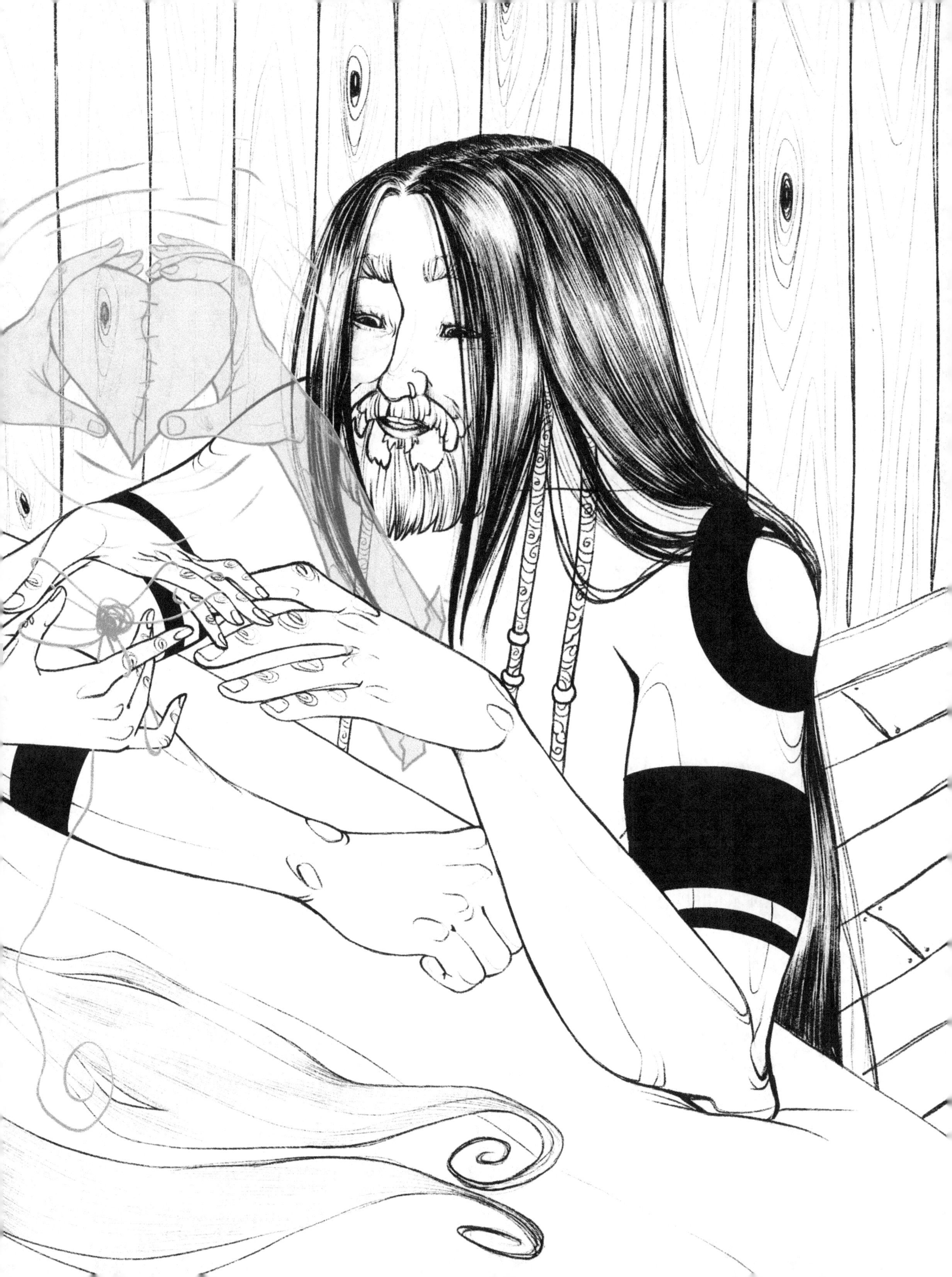

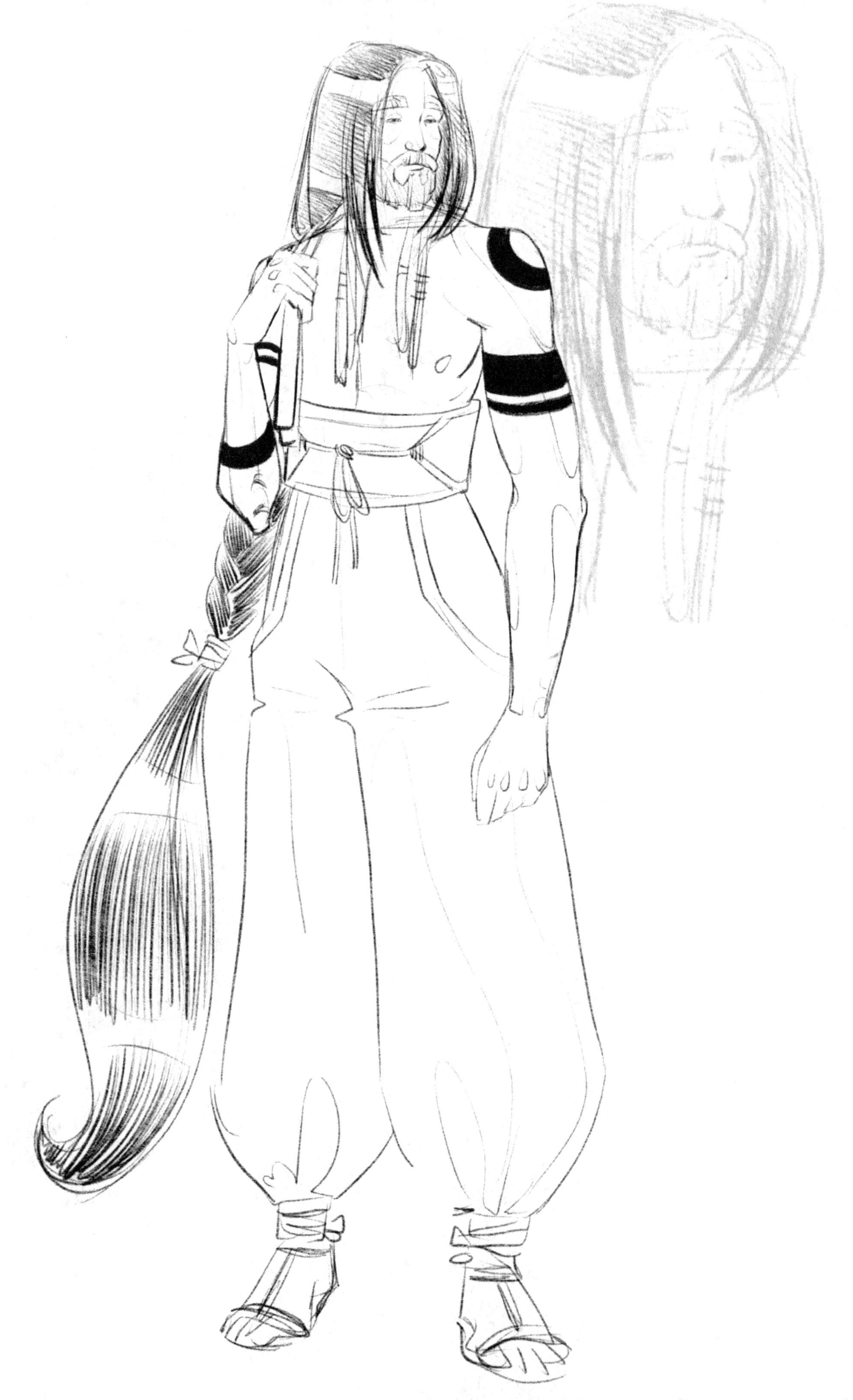

The Fisherman

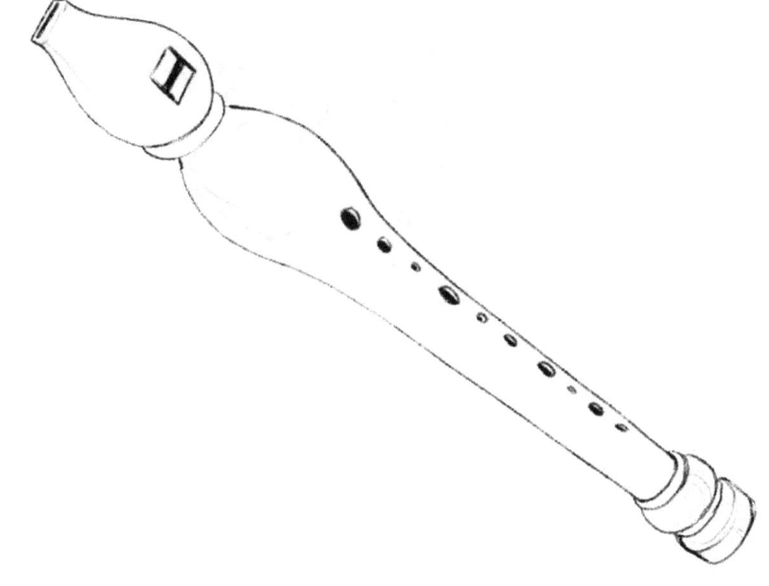

The Lass

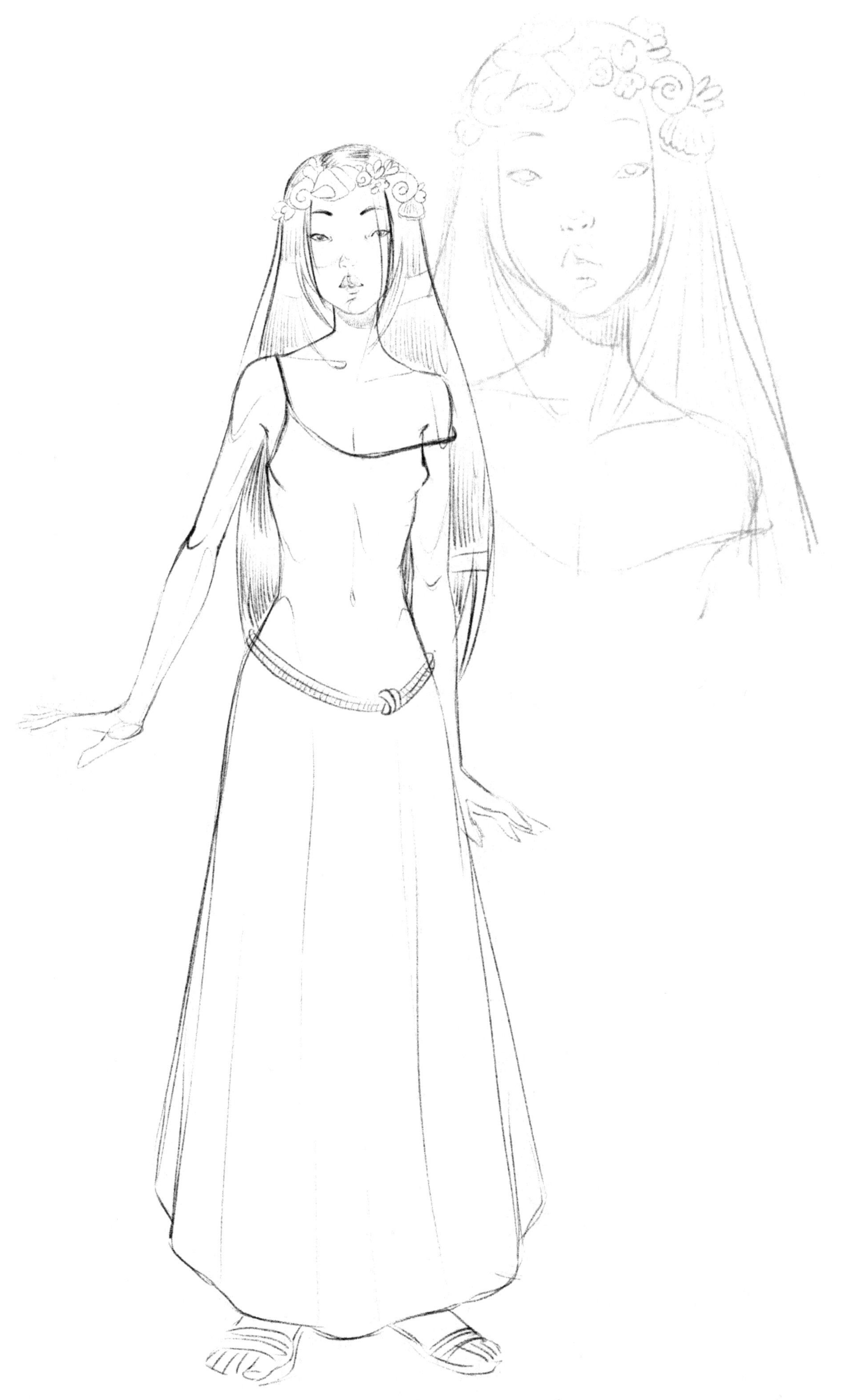

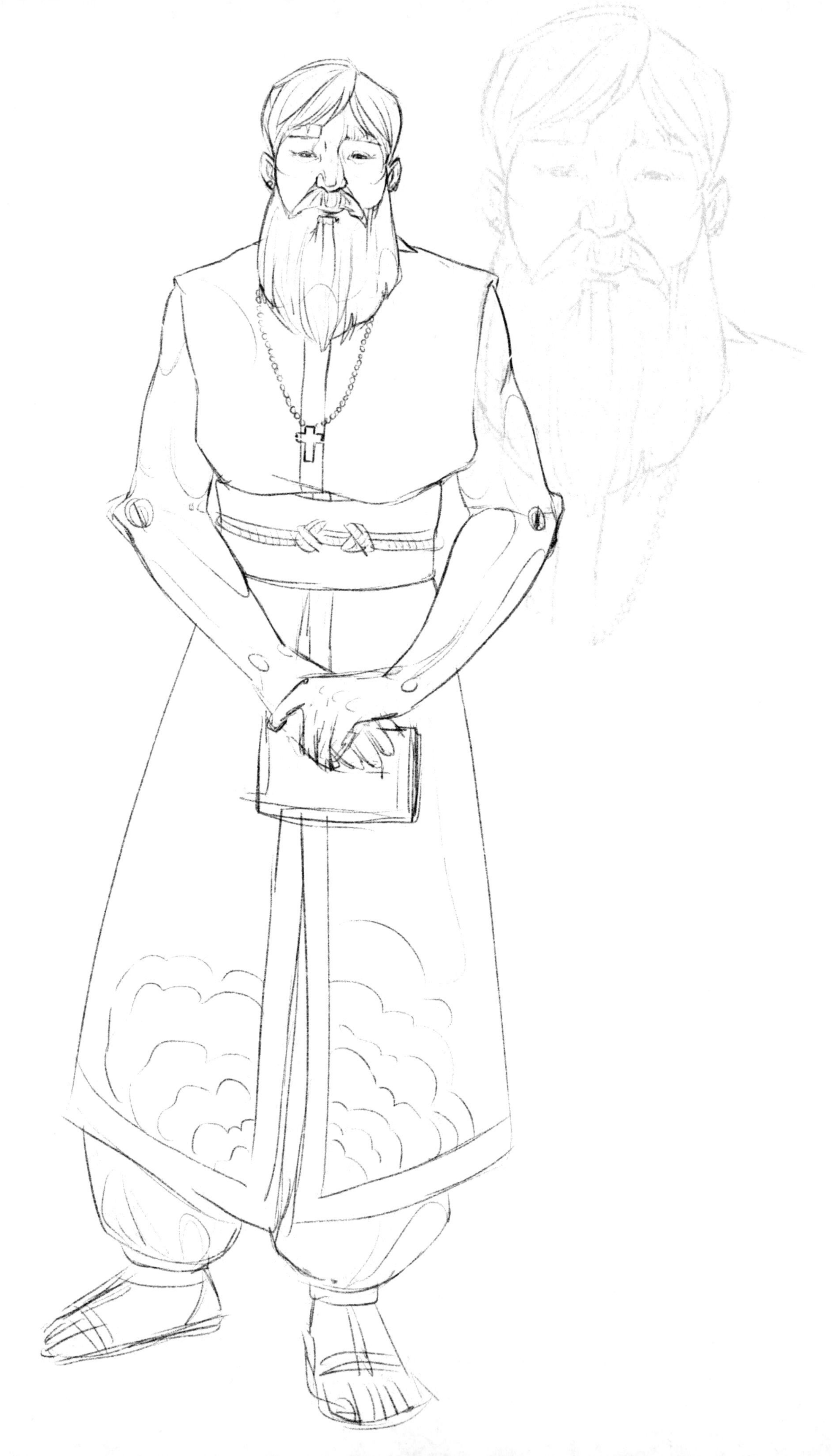

The Preacher

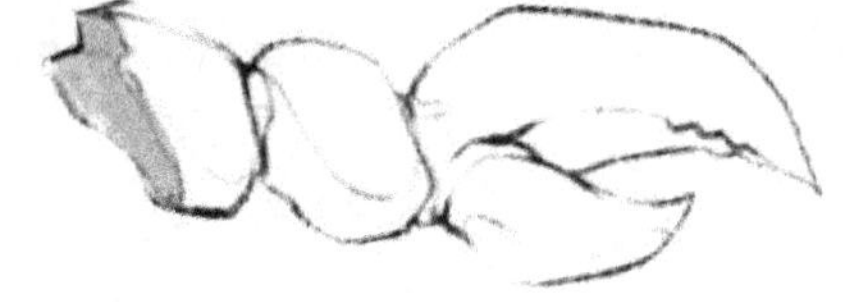